HAUNTED
MICHIGAN
GRAVEYARDS

HAUNTED MICHIGAN GRAVEYARDS

BRADLEY P. MIKULKA

HAUNTED
AMERICA

Published by Haunted America
A Division of The History Press
Charleston, SC
www.historypress.com

All photos by the author.

First published 2023

Manufactured in the United States

ISBN 9781467152501

Library of Congress Control Number: 2023934802

CONTENTS

CONTENTS

INTRODUCTION

Who doesn't love going to a graveyard? You can visit the grave of a loved one or a famous person who is buried there. They are peaceful and quiet. Well, they are usually peaceful.

For whatever reason, however, there are some graveyards where the spirits of the people who are buried there are not resting in peace.

For centuries, there have been stories about some graveyards being haunted. Stories abound of people seeing spirits looking at them or standing near their tombstones, hearing disembodied screams and laughter, seeing shadow figures darting between the tombstones—and the list goes on and on.

For some, the seemingly harmless and sometimes playful antics take on a sinister feel. Unfortunately, there have also been reports over the years of people being pushed and scratched by unseen hands and having things thrown at them and hooded figures chasing people out of graveyards.

Having been a ghost hunter since 1996, I have spent a fair amount of time in graveyards in the state of Michigan. I have experienced a few things during my time there. I still like to visit a good graveyard now and then.

In this book, I will take you to some of the haunted graveyards in the state and tell you some of the stories and encounters that have occurred there. The best thing about these graveyards is that they are open to the public and you can visit them yourselves—and you might even have an encounter or two with a spirit yourself.

But before you go to any of these graveyards yourself or with a friend, and if you are going for the sole purpose of seeing something or of being scared, be careful what you wish for!

CHAPTER 1
BARRY COUNTY

QUAKER CEMETERY, NASHVILLE

Quaker Cemetery is located in the middle of nowhere. It is surrounded by trees and swamps on three of its four sides. There is a long dirt road that leads into the cemetery. I will not lie; the graveyard is hard to find. If you find it, you will have the place to yourself, as there aren't houses or people around for miles. The actual address is 8495 Guy Road. The graveyard itself is pretty small, but there are a few tombstones. Quite a few of the tombstones are old and weathered, making it impossible to read them. There are no hours posted, but you can probably be there as long as you want.

There is a sign at the entrance of the graveyard that reads:

> *Quaker settlement and cemetery between 1836 and 1837. John Mott, a prominent Jackson Quaker, patented 1520 acres in this area. Eli Lapham, a Quaker minister, was the first settler in Maple Grove Township (1837), having purchased land from Mr. Mott. William Sutton and Abram Quick married daughters of Mr. Lapham and settled nearby, Quick erected the first sawmill in the township for Mr. Mott. At one time, there were many residents of the area that were of the Quaker faith, but have long since passed on leaving few traces of their existence beyond the cemetery and Quaker Brook.*

The tombstones to the upper right have bad vibes to them. You will have the feeling of dread and just an overall uneasy feeling. There are trees directly to the east of these tombstones, and you'll have the feeling that you are being watched from these trees.

On the right side of the graveyard is a cluster of three small grave markers. Around these grave markers, one gets the feeling that something is watching you from down the hill. But if you look, there isn't anyone there. You might also have your pant leg pulled, and sometimes you will hear your name called by a disembodied voice.

One of the stories going around is centered on a Revolutionary War soldier. He supposedly patrols the graveyard and guards it against any intruders. He has been seen mainly on the hill in the middle of the graveyard.

Quaker Cemetery is a long-forgotten graveyard, but it is well maintained. If you find this graveyard, beware of the soldier. It has been said that he carries a weapon and will chase you out of the graveyard if you dare to enter. You have been warned!

CHAPTER 2

CALHOUN COUNTY

BATTLE CREEK MEMORIAL PARK, BATTLE CREEK

Battle Creek Memorial Park is located at 2435 West Territorial Road in Battle Creek. One word of advice if you come to this graveyard: the entrance off South Helmer Road is closed. You need to enter from West Territorial Road. There is only one road into the graveyard, but there are many inside the graveyard. It would be hard to give you exact directions to the paranormal spots, so you are kind of on your own to find them once you make it inside. The hours are posted: from dawn to dusk. The whole time we were in the graveyard, it appeared a silver Jeep was shadowing our every move. He was always a ways from us, but when we stopped, he stopped. When we moved, he moved. When we left the graveyard, he was at the front entrance by the office. Just be advised: you may be watched by interested parties if you go there. The graveyard is flanked by Territorial Road to the north, Helmer Road to the west, houses to the east and Columbia Avenue to the south.

One of the more prominent people laid to rest here is Paul Werntz Shafer. He was a U.S. congressman, a newspaper journalist and a publisher. There is also a John Kellogg buried here. I'm not sure if he was part of the Kellogg cereal family, but I would assume that he was. In the southwest corner, there is a mausoleum for John Kellogg. All around here, you get the feeling of being watched, and I do not mean by the person in the silver Jeep. If you take a picture through the door of the mausoleum, you might get an orb.

The John Kellogg Mausoleum, where some activity has been experienced.

On the east side of the graveyard, there are seven rows of tombstones all in a line, laid out in a semicircle. In this area, you will find a small section of land that does not feel right; the area feels a little "off." There is no other way to describe it. When you feel it, you will know what I mean!

In the section over to your left, you might hear some voices. They sound like those of children, but you cannot hear or make out what is being said.

Battle Creek Memorial Park is fairly big. It would be a nice place to visit if you have time to spare, since there are a lot of cool-looking tombstones to see. If the silver Jeep follows you around, ask him what he wants!

HARMON HALLADAY CEMETERY, SPRINGFIELD

Harmon Halladay Cemetery, also known as Harmon Cemetery or Holiday Cemetery, is located at O Drive N in Springfield. This graveyard is north of Waubascon Road. There are no roads that take you into the graveyard. You will need to park on the side of the road. This is a really small graveyard with only a handful of tombstones. If you look closely, however, you can find some markers that lie flat and have been covered over with grass. Some of the tombstones have been displaced by tree roots. There are no hours posted, but I assume you could be there as late as you would like, since there are no current tombstones there. Most of the tombstones are from the 1800s. This graveyard is surrounded by trees to the north, south and east. O Drive N runs to the west of the graveyard. There are trees across the street to the west as well as Calvary Apostolic Church.

There is a tree line directly to the south of the graveyard. If you stand near this tree line, you will have an overwhelming feeling of being watched. It feels like your every move is being watched closely, almost as if someone or something wants to know why you are in this graveyard. You might also hear sobs coming from this same area. It sounds like either a woman or child is making the sound.

Near the north end of the graveyard is a tombstone for a couple named Joseph and Sarah Stall. The tombstone is an interesting one, and near here, you get the feeling of being at peace. A little to the south of this tombstone is one for Henry B. Scidmore. In front of his tombstone, you will get the feeling of anger.

Over near the trees to the east, in a certain area, you will have goosebumps and you will feel like you are not alone, even though you cannot see anyone there. It is possible that there are some unmarked graves in this area and that is why you have that feeling. They do not want to be forgotten.

Harmon Halladay Cemetery is a nice little graveyard. Most of the people laid to rest here do not have family who are still alive. If you visit them, you are keeping their memory alive. There is a Civil War veteran buried here. His name was Dalton Halladay. If you come for a visit, go to his tombstone and render a salute and thank him for his service!

MOUNT OLIVET CEMETERY, BATTLE CREEK

Mount Olivet Cemetery does not have a physical address. It is located on South Avenue south of East Dickman Road. The graveyard's hours are not posted, but I would assume it is open from dawn to dusk. The graveyard borders East Burnham Street to the north, and there is open land to the west, South Avenue to the east and an empty American Stamping building to the south. There is one entrance to the graveyard, and the

Above: In this area, you might have the feeling of dread and sadness.

Opposite: Near this tombstone, an apparition of a nun has been seen.

road then forms a semicircle back to the entrance. There are many tombstones from the 1800s, but there are also some more current ones. The entrance to the cemetery can be a little challenging if you have a vehicle low to the ground. There is a very low clearance, but if you come in at an angle, you should be fine.

When you drive in and follow the road to the right, on your left, there is a monument for the Reverend R.J. Sadlier. To the right of this monument is a tombstone that is covered up with a green tarp. I do not know the reason behind this, but right in front of the covered tombstone, you feel dread and sadness.

If you follow the road around and you are directly behind the monument to the Reverend, a little to your right is a cluster of really old tombstones. It is in this area that you will get the feeling of being sad—so much, in fact, that you might shed a tear or two.

Go up the road a little bit until the monument to the Reverend is to your left. To the northeast a little is a cluster of five older tombstones. You might hear voices and see a ball of light moving in and out of these tombstones.

Near one of the bigger trees is the tombstone for Mother Margret Flood. What looks like a nun, totally transparent, has been seen standing in front of the tombstone of Mother Flood. She has been observed standing for a few seconds and then slowly disappearing.

Mount Olivet Cemetery is a nice Catholic cemetery. It has some interesting tombstones and monuments. If you see the apparition of Mother Flood, let it be. If you happen to find out why the one tombstone right beside the Reverend Sadlier is covered with a green tarp, please let me know. I am more than curious about why this is and what they did to be covered!

Oak Hill Cemetery, Battle Creek

Oak Hill Cemetery is a grand old graveyard located at 255 South Avenue in Battle Creek. The graveyard borders Oak Hill Drive to the north, South Avenue to the west, trees to the south and homes to the east. There is one entrance to the graveyard, and once inside, there are many roads that go in every direction. The graveyard is open from dawn to dusk. There are many distinct types and styles of tombstones, many going back to the 1800s.

Many notable people were laid to rest here. Among them was Julius Granger Fisk, who was a Civil War army officer; Charles Maynard Holton, who earned the Medal of Honor during the Civil War; John Harvey Kellogg, who was a medical pioneer and who coined the term *sanitarium*; and Will Keith Kellogg, who pioneered something you might eat for breakfast, the cornflake.

When you first enter the graveyard, follow the road to the right. You will come upon a huge monument for Winman-Risdon. You cannot miss it; it has a big cross on it, and it will be right in front of you. If you walk down the road to your right, you will come upon a cluster of older veterans' tombstones. It is in this area that a black form has been seen kneeling by one of the tombstones.

If you drive straight ahead, there will be a cool church, with a bell, on your right. If you take the first left past the church and then take a right, you will come upon the newer veterans' section. You cannot miss it, as there will be a flagpole flying Old Glory, and the white tombstones form a circle. A blue ball of light has been seen hovering near these tombstones. It is not seen moving; it just stays in one spot and then disappears.

Continue straight for a few feet; to your northwest is a black tombstone for Wm. J. and Phoebe A. Garfield. An apparition of a man has been seen standing just to the right of the tombstone. He will only appear for a few seconds and then he disappears.

If you head to the east side of the graveyard, you will find the graves of the Kellogg family. You cannot miss the spot, as it has a wrought iron fence around it. In the middle of the plot, there is a pedestal, and on top of it, there is a sundial. There is an inscription that says, "The early bird gets the worm." To the right of this plot, there have been reports of people smelling pipe smoke, even though no one nearby was smoking a pipe.

When you are on the road to leave the graveyard, the same one you came in on, when you see the last right before you leave the graveyard, you might want to stop and walk down the road a little. In front of you, there will be

Above: This is the monument at the Kellogg family burial plot.

Left: Sojourner Truth's tombstone. Some people get goosebumps near here.

a tombstone and plaque. These are for Sojourner Truth. If you don't know who she is, Google her! People have gotten the chills when they walk up to her tombstone. The inscription reads:

> *In Memoriam Sojourner Truth Born a Slave in Ulster Co. N.Y. in the 18th Century Died in Battle Creek Mich.*
> *Nov. 26, 1883, Died About 105 Years "Is God Dead"*

There is a plaque beside her tombstone that reads:

> *Sojourner Truth, renowned lecturer and reformer who championed anti-slavery, rights of women and the freedmen, rests here. Beside her lie two of her five children.*

Oak Hill Cemetery has a lot of history. There are quite a few prominent people buried here. If you happen to see Mr. Kellogg, let him know his cereal is great! If you see the spirit of a veteran, thank him for his service. And lastly, if you see Sojourner Truth, let her rest in peace; she deserves it.

REESE CEMETERY, SPRINGFIELD

Reese Cemetery is located at 351 North Thirty-Fourth Street in Springfield. There are two entrances to the graveyard. The main one is off West Dickman Road. The other entrance is in the northeast corner off North Thirty-Fourth Street and Shetler Street. The graveyard borders Dickman Road to the south, Helmer Road to the west, trees to the north and open land to the east. There are many different time frames for the dates on the tombstones. There are some current dates and some going back as far as the 1800s. The posted hours that the graveyard is open are from dawn to dusk.

If you make your way to the northwest corner of the graveyard, you are in what I think is the veteran's section. There is a flagpole that has Old Glory flying from it. In this area, there are veterans' tombstones. If you walk across the road to the south, there is a cluster of veterans' tombstones also. I am not sure why, but there have been reports in this area of people being touched and scratched. There have also been voices heard in this area when there is not anyone around.

If you go to the northeast of the veteran's section, you will come across the tombstone of William T. Baggs. It is around this area that you might catch a whiff of freshly tilled earth, even though nothing has been disturbed.

Just a little to the northeast of the veteran's section, you will find one lone tree. Under the tree, to the right, is a marker for D.B. Voorheis. An apparition of a man has been seen standing right in front of his marker. The apparition looks down at the marker and then slowly fades away.

Reese Cemetery is a nice graveyard to visit. If you happen to see the spirit of a veteran, thank him for his service. If you happen to see the apparition of the man standing by Mr. Voorheis's marker, and you get the chance, ask him his name. I would be interested to know if it was Mr. Voorheis. Thanks in advance!

YOUNG'S CEMETERY, BATTLE CREEK

Young's Cemetery, a.k.a Goguac Cemetery, is not even listed on Google Maps. It is near the corner of West Territorial Road and South Thirty-First Street. The graveyard butts up against Battle Creek Memorial Park to the west, Territorial Road to the north, Thirty-First Street to the east and houses to the south. The graveyard is just to the west of the Hangar Party Store. There are two entrances to the graveyard off Territorial Road, and the road into the graveyard forms a *U*. There is a chain-link fence surrounding the graveyard. There are no hours posted, but since there is a gate, I would

Near these two tombstones, people have reported being pushed.

assume the hours are from dawn to dusk. There do not seem to be any recent burials, and most of the tombstones date to the 1800s. There are a few that are hard to read because they are so weathered from being out in the elements all these years.

In the middle of the graveyard is a tombstone for Henry C. Eberstein. Near his tombstone, there have been reports of people smelling cigar smoke when no one in the area was smoking. There is also a tombstone for Alice V. Edmonds where people have caught the smell of roses when there were not any roses in the graveyard.

In the north part of the cemetery, just off the road, is a pair of tombstones, both impossible to read because they are so old. There have been reports that some people have been pushed in this area when there was not anyone there to push them. Also in this area, people have heard whispers and felt that they were being watched.

Young's Cemetery is a well-kept smaller graveyard. If you come to this graveyard, be on the lookout for Henry and Alice. If you happen to see their spirits, tell them "Hi" for me. Thanks!

CHAPTER 3

CHIPPEWA COUNTY

MISSION HILL, BRIMLEY

Mission Hill is located on top of a hill in the Upper Peninsula of Michigan, north of Brimley. There is no address listed on Google Maps, but the graveyard is located on West Tower Road off West Lakeshore Drive. Be advised that the road leading up to the graveyard is a narrow, one-lane road with a gradual incline. The graveyard is surrounded on all four sides by trees. There are trees on one side of the road and a drop-off on the other. Two cars can pass each other on the road, but barely. There is a sign before you start the trek up to the graveyard that reads, "RVs not recommended on this road." Many of the tombstones are handmade, and the majority of them are for Native Americans. The hours are not listed, but I would assume you can be there anytime within reason.

When you get to the top of the hill on the left, you'll find the entrance to the graveyard. But on the right, there is a small parking area to enjoy the view. Its official name is Mission Hill Cemetery Scenic Overlook. This looks down on Spectacle Lake. I would highly recommend taking in the view before you enter the graveyard. For a bonus, visit during the fall colors. You won't be disappointed!

As you enter the graveyard, the first thing you will notice is how quiet it is. Because of its location on top of a hill, there isn't anything around that would create noise. The second thing that will strike you is that the

Sailors from the steamer *Myron* are laid to rest here.

graveyard is surrounded on all sides by trees. The only breaks are the two roads that lead out of the cemetery.

A little side note: there is a lot of wildlife in the graveyard. Squirrels and chipmunks can be seen frolicking between the tombstones.

There have been reports of and pictures taken that show a black shadow form in the shape of a child that has been seen kneeling over graves as if it was paying its respects. Other people have seen a man dressed in all black with his arms crossed, leaning against a fence.

There aren't any so-called famous people buried here. However, it is hard not to notice the white picket fence that surrounds one tombstone. This is the final resting place for eight crewmembers of the *Steamer Myron*. There is a plaque by the fence that reads:

> *Sailors of the Steamer Myron*
> *During the early evening of November 22, 1919, the Steamer Myron slid beneath the waves of Lake Superior off Whitefish Point during a violent storm. The crew attempted to use the lifeboats while the Captain chose to remain with his ship. The crew perished but the Captain was found near Ile Parisienne, clinging to a portion of the floating wreckage. In the spring of 1920, eight bodies from the Myron, encased in ice, washed ashore at Salt Point.*
> *They are buried here. May they Rest in Peace.*

The reason I mention the *Myron* at length is that I had a story told to me by a family friend who was in the graveyard a few years ago. This is the story I was told:

> *The husband and I were in the graveyard and we were just looking around. They were talking about the Myron, but couldn't find the plaque or tombstone. At the time, they didn't know that the white picket fence surrounded the tombstone of the crewmembers. Our friend said that she looked to her right and there was an older woman dressed in Native American clothing. The older woman looked at her and pointed in the direction of the white picket fence and said, "What you are looking for is over there." Our friend said that she looked in the direction that the old woman had pointed and saw the white picket fence. She looked back to thank her, and the old woman was gone. Our friend said that she looked around and didn't see the old woman. There was no way that the old woman could have left the graveyard that fast without being seen. She asked her husband where the old woman went. He replied, "What old woman? What are you talking about?" He never saw her.*

Now, I cannot guarantee that if you take a trip to Mission Hill you will encounter either the older Native American woman or the man leaning against the fence—or for that matter, the childlike form. But I can't say that you won't!

Mission Hill Cemetery is a nice graveyard if you want to see some good examples of homemade tombstones and monuments. If you do venture up there, I would recommend stopping at the Dancing Crane Coffee House on West Lakeshore Drive, just a few miles south of the graveyard. It is a Native American–owned business. They have hot chocolate that is to die for—pun intended!

CHAPTER 4
CLINTON COUNTY

BLOOD CEMETERY, LAINGSBURG

Blood Cemetery is located at 9098 Jason Road #9068. There have been stories about Blood Cemetery for years. The cemetery itself isn't very big. A wrought iron fence surrounds the cemetery, and there is a caretaker's building located in the right-hand corner. Like those of most cemeteries, Blood Cemetery's hours are from dawn to dusk. Just a word of advice if you go after dark, while no one will come and close the gate, effectively locking you in, there are neighbors across the street who keep an eye on the cemetery. They will not hesitate to call the police. You have been warned!

Blood Cemetery is an ominous name. The first thing that comes to mind is maybe a murder, a sacrifice or something else sinister. Truth be told, the cemetery is named after a prominent family in the area, the Bloods. The father was a doctor and practiced in the area. The name Dr. Blood, one would assume, scared his patients!

The first thing you will notice as you enter the cemetery is a tall, white monument. This is the tombstone for the Blood family. It lists, I believe, all the Blood family members who are buried there. The monument, as you would expect, is very weathered and hard to read. The dates appear to be from the 1800s to the early 1900s.

As mentioned before, there have been many stories about Blood Cemetery. These stories were way before the Internet and Google and passed on from person to person. As is normally the case with any story passed down, you don't know if the stories are true. But then again, you don't know if they aren't! The following are some of the stories about Blood Cemetery.

It seems that the doctor killed his wife and cut her up into pieces. To avoid getting caught and maybe going to jail, he went into the cemetery and hanged himself. It has been reported that some people who visited at night have seen an armless old lady wearing a red dress who disappears into the mist. On certain occasions, the doctor has also made an appearance near the tree that he supposedly hanged himself from.

There also have been stories that happened near one tombstone in the cemetery. The sounds of growling can be heard, and glowing red eyes have been seen near this tombstone. If you walk near this tombstone, you will feel like someone is watching you, and a sudden, unexplained coldness will surround you. If you walk away from this tombstone, you lose that feeling of being watched, and the coldness suddenly goes away.

There is an old barn directly to the west of the cemetery, outside of the fence. Sometime in the late 1970s, a couple of teenage boys went into the cemetery at night. They saw something that scared them so much that they immediately left the cemetery. A couple of days later, one of the boys was found dead in the barn; he had hanged himself from the rafters. To this day, people have reported seeing the spirit of a teenage boy coming from the barn into the cemetery. It is said that he walks right through the fence and disappears shortly thereafter.

The main story is something that happened in the early 1980s. It seems that a group of five teenagers went to the cemetery one night and parked their car in the cemetery. They were sitting either on their car or on the ground near it and telling scary stories, trying to scare each other. They abruptly left the cemetery, and they crashed a few miles down the road. They all died but one girl. The police visited her in the hospital, and she told them what happened. She died shortly after the interview.

The girl said that she and four other friends decided to go to Blood Cemetery on Saturday night because they were bored and looking for something to do. They drove the car into the cemetery and parked. They were sitting around telling ghost stories when, during one of the stories, they heard a growling sound coming from somewhere inside the cemetery— remember, one of the previous stories was about hearing a growling sound. She said that they could not tell where it came from. They looked around and didn't see anything, so they all thought they had just imagined it, being in a cemetery at night and all.

The girl said that when another friend started telling another story, they heard the same growling sound, but this time they also heard a noise that sounded like someone moving around them. They were getting freaked out and decided to leave. They all got into the car and started to drive off. But the car wouldn't move. They put the car in reverse and drive a few times, but the car wouldn't move.

The girl said that someone looked out the back window and saw a creature about eight feet tall with glowing red eyes holding the back of the car. They all screamed and were all freaking out. Finally, they got the car going and sped out of the cemetery. They turned left onto Jason Road and then left onto South Hollister Road. They looked out the back window and saw that the creature was following them!

They turned right onto round Lake Road heading toward 127; they were speeding, trying to get away from the creature that was still following them. They went through a red light on 127 and were hit by an eighteen-wheeler.

Blood Cemetery is a place you must go to if you can. But I would strongly suggest that you go with a friend. The story goes that if you go by yourself, you might not ever be seen alive again.

DEWITT CITY CEMETERY, DEWITT

Dewitt City Cemetery is located at 801 North Bridge Street in Dewitt. This graveyard is open from dawn to dusk. The graveyard has nine entrances off North Bridge Street, and it consists of ten parcels, which makes this a large cemetery. The graveyard has trees to the east and houses to the north and south, and North Bridge Street runs its length to the west.

According to a sign in the graveyard, this graveyard is a City of Dewitt Historic Site. The sign states:

> *Originally the private burial grounds for the Scott family, this cemetery was made public by the Scotts in 1841. As one of the oldest burial grounds in the county, it is the resting place of many veterans from the War of 1812, the Civil War, and the "Toledo War."*

There are a couple of victims from the Bath School bombing buried here. Also buried here is Randolph Strickland, a U.S. congressman. There is a

Medal of Honor recipient from World War II buried here; his name was Oscar G. Johnson.

If you take the fourth entrance into the cemetery, there will be quite a few trees. In this area, there have been reports of bright white orbs darting between the trees. Also, in this area, you might hear what sounds like a child's laughter.

Continue straight on this road and take a left at the *T*. Go north and take a left at the fourth road. If you stop as soon as you turn, in this area, you might hear a child's laughter again. People have put toys down by the child's tombstone only to find that when they come back a short time later, the toy has been moved, and there is no one else in the graveyard who could have moved it.

Take the road toward Bridge Street and stop just before you get to the main road; there have been sightings of a white, fairly large mist that hovers in one area. You might also feel a cold spot in this area as well as the sensation of being watched.

Go out to Bridge Street and take a left, go to the last road at the end of the cemetery and take another left. Follow the road till it curves around back to the north. Continue driving north, and when the road again curves, stop here. In this area, there have been reports of the paranormal. Even though this section of the graveyard only has a few tombstones, there has been sightings of something, never really seen clearly, peeking out from the third row of trees. When you go and investigate, nothing can be found.

Dewitt City Cemetery is fairly large. You can spend many hours walking through this graveyard looking at the different tombstones. If you visit this graveyard and come across Mr. Johnson, thank him for his service!

Essex Township Cemetery, Maple Rapids

Essex Township Cemetery doesn't have an address according to Google Maps, but it is located on the corner of West Island Road and Essex Center Road southeast of Maple Rapids. Even though the hours are not posted, I would suspect that the graveyard is open from dawn to dusk. It is surrounded by fields, and there are a few trees scattered along the sides of the graveyard. There don't seem to be older or newer sections here; tombstones of all ages are mixed. There are a couple of houses to the east of the cemetery. The main driveway into the graveyard will take you to the front of the only mausoleum in the graveyard.

In front of the mausoleum, people have recorded EVPs telling them to "get out" and had the general feeling of being watched. There have also been cold spots reported on the north and east sides of the mausoleum.

The road just in front of the mausoleum seems to be a hot spot in the cemetery. There have been reports of being watched and moving cold spots in this area. People have stated that when walking in this area, they felt like someone was walking right behind them. When they turned around, there was no one there.

Essex Township Cemetery is a rather small graveyard out in the countryside and would be a nice little graveyard to visit. If you are planning a visit to the area, right in front of the mausoleum seems like the place to start. Good luck.

EUREKA CEMETERY, ST. JOHNS

Eureka Cemetery is located at 2194 East Hyde Road. The graveyard is actually on both sides of the road. If you're heading east, the newer section is on the left and the older section is on the right. There are four entrances

Near these veterans' tombstones, a black human form has been seen.

to the north section and three entrances to the south section. The dates on the tombstones are from the 1800s to the present. The hours are from dawn to dusk. The older section has quite a few tombstones of Civil War soldiers.

In the newer section, a man dressed in all brown, much like a UPS driver, will suddenly appear and will carry on a conversation with you. After a few minutes, while you are not looking at him, as suddenly as he appeared, he will suddenly just disappear. There is no place for him to have gone in that short period of time.

In the older section of the graveyard, a black, humanlike form has been seen near the cluster of Civil War tombstones. He has been observed looking down toward the ground. When you try to approach him, he will slowly fade away until he is gone.

Not far from the Civil War tombstones is a cluster of trees. Around these trees, there have been reports of people having an uneasy feeling and the feeling of being watched. There also have been cold spots around this area.

Eureka Cemetery is a nice, well-maintained graveyard that is worth a visit if you are a Civil War buff, since there are a few veterans of that war laid to rest there. If you go to this graveyard and happen to see the humanlike figure near the tombstones, see if you can communicate with him. Try and get a name; we need to figure out who this is so we can place a name to him.

FAIRFIELD CEMETERY, ELSIE

Fairfield Cemetery is a large graveyard that is located on both sides of the road. Google Maps does not seem to want to give this graveyard an actual address, so this graveyard is located on North Vincent Road off West Juddville Road. The west section of the graveyard has five entrances off North Vincent Road. Only two plots have tombstones, while the three plots to the north are empty, I would assume for further burials. The east section only has one entrance, and the road stops near the east side of the graveyard. You have to carefully back up and get back on the road to leave the graveyard. The graveyard has open fields and one lone house to the west, trees and open land to the north and trees to the east and south. The dates of the tombstones range from the 1800s to the present day. The hours are from dawn to dusk.

If you turn into the east section and follow the road till it stops, carefully back up so as not to hit any tombstones and pull ahead just a little so you are facing North Vincent Road. In this area, on the right, near the monument for Scott, an apparition of a man has been seen. He has been described as being in his twenties and seen wearing a baseball hat, a plaid shirt and jeans.

On the right, near the center of the graveyard, you will see a tree and a bush. Nestled in between them, you will see a tombstone for Wilase, or close to it—the tombstone is badly weathered and hard to read. Directly in front of this tombstone, you might feel incredible sadness, and you might get goosebumps. You also will get the undeniable feeling that you are not alone there and that a spirit that you cannot see is there with you.

If you cross North Vincent Road to the west section, make sure you enter the first road to the south. Before you take the curve, there will be a couple of trees and bushes on your left. In this area, and to the south, you will see two tombstones. Near here, you might hear what sounds like the low sobbing of a woman. One lone orb has also been seen in this area. As in some of the other graveyards in this book, electronic equipment has a hard time working correctly here. Cameras sometimes will not take pictures. You press down on the shutter button, but nothing happens. However, if you ask permission to take a picture and press down on the shutter button, you will be able to take a picture!

Follow the curve, and in front of you on your left will be a building I assume is for the caretakers. Directly to the south of this building is a cluster of tombstones. In this general area, you might get an EVP of a man's voice talking in a low whisper. You can never make out what is being said, but you can hear it.

There is a tree a little to the left of these tombstones. There are a couple of tombstones beside the tree. Here, you might feel like you are being watched and that something unseen is standing next to you.

Fairfield Cemetery is a nice graveyard with room for expansion. If you visit and happen to see the man with the baseball hat, if you would, ask him his last name. It might start with an *S*, and if you could confirm that, I would be appreciative! Also, if you get an EVP in the west section of a man, and if you can make out what he is saying, let me know!

FORD CEMETERY, ELSIE

Ford Cemetery is a large, well-maintained graveyard that is located at 111067, 11253 East South Gratiot Co. Line Road. There are no fewer than seven entrances to the graveyard. The graveyard is surrounded by trees to the south and open land to the west, north and east. The graveyard has tombstones from the early 1800s to the present. The hours are from dawn to dusk.

If you are heading east, you will want to take the first entrance. There will be a building in front of you. Just past the curve and on your right, there has been some activity noted: verified cold spots and the feeling of being touched. Nothing threatening, just a tug on your shirt, as if someone was trying to get your attention.

Continue straight and past the first intersection. Be on the lookout for the lone bush on your left. It will be the only bush near the road in this whole section. Nestled in the bush is a white tombstone that is shaped like a cross near the top and has rosary beads engraved on it hanging from the cross. The name on it is Dudash. In this immediate vicinity, you will most likely get a headache. Your head will feel like it is about ready to explode. I mean, it will not, but it feels like your head is in a vice! As soon as you walk away from this area, the headache is gone!

People near this tombstone have reported getting headaches.

Near this cluster of tombstones, people have recorded EVPs.

Directly across the road to your left is a tombstone for Smith. The tombstone is vertical and is a granite color. It has a big concrete base. Around the tombstone, there has been a sighting of the apparition of a woman. She has been described as an older lady with short white hair and chubby cheeks, wearing glasses, something similar to stretch pants and a floral shirt.

If you are brave enough to experience some more paranormal stuff, follow this road until it curves. On your left, you will see a cluster of trees. A little to the right of these trees, you will see a tall, white obelisk monument for Smith. In front of this, there are three tombstones, all weathered. In this area, there have been reports of feeling watched, cold spots and getting an EVP of a man's voice saying, "Help me." Orbs have also been seen in this area.

Let us try something a little different. I am going to send you on a scavenger hunt in this graveyard! Somewhere in the graveyard—I am not going to tell you where—you will find a white tombstone with a lamb that is lying down on it. In this general area, an apparition of a child has been seen! The child is a boy and has been seen wearing short pants—maybe they could be shorts—a white button-down shirt and a hat. He has been observed standing in front of this tombstone and looking at it.

Ford Cemetery is a nice graveyard worthy of a visit with room for expansion. If you do visit and see the little old lady, try to get her name and let me know what it is. I am fairly sure I know what her name is, but I would like verification! If you find the tombstone in the little scavenger hunt, please tell the little boy it is OK to move on! And last but not least, be sure to bring some aspirin for the headache you will probably get!

HURD CEMETERY, LANSING

Hurd Cemetery is a quaint little graveyard that has no actual address, at least not according to Google Maps. The graveyard is located south of Dewitt on Dewitt Road just before West Stoll Road. There are two entrances off Dewitt Road. The graveyard has houses to the south and trees to the west and north. There is a church that sits in front of the graveyard and faces Dewitt Road. The dates on the tombstones are from the 1800s to the present. There are no hours posted, but I would think it would be safe to state that they are from dawn to dusk.

The graveyard has tombstones that date back to the 1800s. There is a tombstone for "Hurd," and I assume this is who the graveyard is named after. There are some very interesting tombstones here, and I would be interested in finding out the thought behind them.

If you enter the graveyard from the first entrance closest to West Stoll Road, follow the driveway around the curve, continue back toward Dewitt Road, stop halfway and park, you will be near where there have been reports of activity.

If you walk north, you will see another driveway and some pine trees. Near this driveway is one particularly big tree. There is a tombstone right beside this tree, to the west, and the name on the tombstone is Felzke. In this area, there have been reports—or should it be a smell—of perfume. The perfume is said to smell like lavender, so you can assume it is a woman's perfume. There are pine trees in the area, but the perfume smells like lavender, not pine.

After you smell the perfume, you get the feeling that you are not alone. You have the very distinct feeling that something unseen is near you. So close, in fact, that some people have had goosebumps on their arms during the encounter!

To the north of this area is a tombstone that has three tiers and a rather big ball on top. It is in front of this tombstone that an apparition has

This is the area where you might smell lavender flowers when none are around.

This is the spot where the apparition of a man has been seen.

been seen standing with its head bowed. You only see a very quick glimpse before it is gone.

Hurd Cemetery is a graveyard that has a very pleasant feel to it. If you are out driving around and are looking for someplace to visit, I would highly recommend this little graveyard. Walk around and see if you can smell the lavender perfume. If you do catch a whiff, try and find out who the scent belongs to; I am curious!

MAPLE GROVE CEMETERY, OVID

Maple Grove Cemetery is a large graveyard located at 275 East Elm Street. The graveyard has an entrance off East Elm Street and one off M-21. There are houses to the west, an open field to the east, East Elm Street to the north and M-21 to the south. The tombstones range from the 1800s to the 2000s. The hours are dawn to dusk.

If you come in off East Elm Road, take a right and follow the curve, you will see a set of cannons near a flagpole. The cannons were erected in 1898. On one cannon, the inscription reads,

> *In Memoriam of the*
> *Soldiers and Sailors*
> *Who fought in defense of the Union*

Around these cannons has been observed an apparition of a man in military uniform. You cannot make out the branch, but he has been seen mainly around the cannon on the right. He just stands in one spot and looks out over the graveyard.

If you continue straight to the second left, before you come to the next road, there is a cluster of trees on your right. In this area, there have been reports of feeling cold spots and the feeling of being watched. Orbs have also been seen in this area, weaving around the tombstones.

In the center of the graveyard, you will see a mausoleum for Campbell-Pengra. This mausoleum is an interesting one, to say the least. An orb has been seen in the area of this mausoleum; after a few minutes, the orb appears to go to the door of the mausoleum and enter through the closed doors. No one has ever been close enough to the mausoleum to tell for sure if the orb enters the mausoleum, but from a distance, that is what appears to happen.

There has also been an apparition of a woman seen in this area. She has been observed wearing a black dress with a veil over her face.

If you get on the road closest to East Elm Street, follow it around toward the south. You will see a building on your left. In this area, between the building and the road you are on, you might see the black shadow that has been observed crossing the road. It is coming from the building and heading into the graveyard. People have also seen orbs in this area and encountered moving cold spots.

If you enter the graveyard off M-21, you will see a lone tree on your left near the road. There will be a cluster of eight tombstones to the left of this tree. Orbs have been seen in and around these tombstones. The feeling of being watched has also been reported in this area. Video cameras have also malfunctioned in this area. They will seem to work as they should in all other parts of this graveyard. If you play back the video, however, the audio part is perfectly fine, you can hear the sound just fine—but the video is all black.

Maple Grove Cemetery is a nice, well-maintained graveyard. Like most of the other graveyards in this book, some of the spirits here have decided not to rest in peace! If you visit and happen to see the military man by the cannons, thank him for his service. If you are lucky enough to catch a glimpse of the woman in the veil, and if you are brave enough to approach her, kindly get her name and ask what she wants. And let me know what you find out!

MAPLE RAPIDS CEMETERY, MAPLE RAPIDS

Maple Rapids Cemetery is so small and so old that it doesn't even show up on Google Maps. The graveyard doesn't even have a name, so I am calling it Maple Rapids Cemetery. There are no signs posted, so I am not sure of the hours. You can probably be there as late as you wish. The graveyard is located in Maple Rapids at the end of Washington Street, which dead-ends at the graveyard. There are no roads into the graveyard; you simply just walk in. The graveyard is surrounded on three sides by houses and trees to the east. There don't seem to be any recent tombstones; most of them date back to the 1800s. Because of the age of this graveyard, it could be assumed that some of the founding fathers of Maple Rapids are buried here.

There is a tall tombstone in the southeast corner of the graveyard. The name on the tombstone is Adelaide Johnson; she passed in 1856. In the area,

This may be the tombstone of a founding family; people have felt they were being watched near this area.

you will sometimes feel an overwhelming sense of sadness. You might also get the feeling of being watched. One could argue that the feeling could be coming from the houses that surround the graveyard, but the feeling of being watched comes from the tree line to the east.

Near the center of the graveyard, you will find three tall tombstones with a smaller one just to the left. Near here, you will sometimes hear a child's laughter. The laughter sounds like it is coming from directly behind the tombstone on the right. You might also get the sensation of having your pant legs tugged on, almost like a child is trying to get your attention.

One of the houses that borders the graveyard has recorded strange things in the graveyard with its outdoor cameras. The inhabitants have seen a white mist roaming the graveyard and three white lights that dart between the tombstones, like children chasing each other or maybe playing hide and go seek. They have captured these images over the years.

A black form has been observed in the graveyard near the tree line. It will occasionally be seen standing in one spot. It never moves and then it slowly disappears.

Near here, you may hear a child's laughter or have your pant leg tugged.

Maple Rapids Cemetery is an older graveyard located in town; I would assume that some of the people laid to rest here were founding fathers, or at least founding families, of the town. If you visit this graveyard, be alert for anything paranormal. It appears that this little graveyard is an active one. Maybe you can join them in a game of hide and go seek!

MOUNT REST CEMETERY, STREET. JOHNS

Mount Rest Cemetery is located at 701 East Steel Street. The graveyard is open from dawn to dusk. The graveyard has three entrances off East Steel Street and two off East Gibbs Street. There are older tombstones mixed in with newer ones. The graveyard is surrounded by commercial buildings to the west, a subdivision to the north, houses to the east and a few houses but mainly open land to the south.

There is a Civil War veteran, Oliver Lyman Spaulding, buried here, as well as brothers who died in the Bath School bombing. The person responsible for the school bombing is also buried here, in an unmarked grave in the paupers' section of the graveyard.

Once you enter the graveyard, take the first right and then the first left. A little ways on your right will be a mausoleum. Near here, balls of light have been seen. They will move away from the mausoleum, stop and then continue straight until they disappear from view.

If you continue straight on this road, take the first right, and when you come to the first left, take it and drive only a few feet and then stop. If you walk a little bit to your left, you are in the general area where you might hear two people having a conversation. You can't make out what is being said, but two distinct voices can be heard.

Continue straight on the road until the *T*. Turn right and go halfway to East Gibbs Street. On your left, there has been quite a bit of activity. Walk west and go about halfway to the street, which is North Traver Street. A full-bodied apparition, completely transparent, has been seen pacing in this area. The apparition has been described as a male, and he doesn't acknowledge that you are there. He will pace for a short time and then disappear from view. There have also been cases where people have been scratched while in this area. Most of the scratches seem to occur on the arms.

If you walk a little bit to the south, cross the road. Walk past the trees till you see a tree on your left that is all by itself. Here you might encounter the woman in white. She appears hazy, but there is no doubt that she is a woman. Her dress flows behind her as she walks. There is also a feeling that you are not welcome in this area.

Mount Rest Cemetery is a grand ole graveyard with a good example of early styles of tombstones. If you visit this graveyard, the section toward the east doesn't seem to be active. The middle and west side seem to be where the action is. If you happen to see the apparition of the man pacing, if you get a chance, ask him what his name is!

North Eagle Cemetery, Eagle

North Eagle Cemetery is located at 12300 South Grange Road, Eagle. There are numerous entrances to the graveyard. The graveyard is bordered by trees to the south, farmland to the east and north and South Grange Road to the west. There is a house across the street. There is an older section in the center of the graveyard with most of the tombstones dating to the 1800s.

A Michigan Historic Marker in the graveyard.

In front of the graveyard, there is a Michigan Historic Site sign that says, "Joshua Simmons II." Joshua Simmons II, Revolutionary War veteran, is buried in this cemetery. He was born on a Massachusetts farm in the early 1760s. In 1778, he volunteered to fight the British and served with various units in Massachusetts for about two years. In 1790, he married Ruth Andrews. Later, the family migrated to western New York. His wife died in 1806, leaving Joshua to raise their eight children. In the 1830s, his younger son David settled in this area. Joshua joined him and, at his death in 1840, was buried here on his son's land.

There have been what sounds like children laughing heard near the back of the graveyard. Others have heard whispers near the older section of the graveyard. There is a caretaker's building at the north end of the graveyard. A shadow figure has been seen near the tombstones to the left of the building.

A shadowlike figure has been seen crossing the road in front of the cemetery. It is always seen entering the graveyard but never leaving.

North Eagle Cemetery is a historic graveyard that is worthy of a visit. If you visit this graveyard, please pay your respects to Joshua Simmons II; I think he deserves it! I will have to find Mr. Simmons's tombstone on my next visit to properly pay my respects.

PLEASANT HILL CEMETERY, BATH

Pleasant Hill Cemetery is located at 14378 Webster Road. The graveyard is a pretty good-sized one; it covers two city blocks easily. The graveyard is surrounded by trees to the west, a few houses to the north, Webster Road to the east and the Bath Township offices to the south. Its hours are from dawn to dusk. The dates of the tombstones range from the 1800s to the present. Several victims of the 1927 Bath school bombing are laid to rest here.

A few years ago, a man was walking through the cemetery with a couple of his friends. They weren't looking for anything in particular, just taking in the area. He said that when they were in the center of the cemetery, he felt something burning on his back. He didn't think anything of it, but after a few minutes, the burning sensation increased. He had one of his friends lift his shirt, and on his back were three fresh scratch marks. There was a little trickle of blood, so they were fresh rather than old scratch marks.

If you travel down Webster Road heading south, take the next-to-last driveway into the graveyard. When you come to the end, turn right and immediately stop and park. The tall tombstone directly in front of you has been known to be hot, even at night, while other tombstones surrounding it are cool to the touch.

There is a flagpole in the center of the graveyard. To the northwest of this flagpole, black shadows have been observed. They have been seen darting in and around the tombstones. People have also experienced cold spots and the feeling of being watched in this area.

Also, if you go northwest from the flagpole, continue until you cross a driveway. This is the area where voices and children's laughter can be heard. There are houses to the north, but the voices and laughter are heard directly from this area and not off in the distance.

Recently, a news crew from a local TV station was in the cemetery at night doing a segment for Halloween. They observed a green ball of light following one of the crew members around the graveyard. The cameraman saw it through the lens of the camera, but when he looked in the direction of where the green ball of light was, he couldn't see it.

Pleasant Hill Cemetery is a quiet and well-kept graveyard. The graveyard is patrolled at night by the police since some of the victims of the Bath school bombing are buried here. Even though the Bath school bombing happened long ago, it is still a sore subject for the locals. As always, treat this and other graveyards with the respect that they deserve and demand.

REED CEMETERY, LAINGSBURG

Reed Cemetery is located at 6770 Alward Road. The cemetery is in the country and is surrounded by cornfields on the west, south and east and Alward Road to the north. There is a white church in front of the cemetery. Two driveways take you into the cemetery. The dates on the tombstones range from the 1800s to the present. The hours are from dawn to dusk.

The sound of a dog barking has been heard near this tombstone.

If you take the road to the right once you enter the graveyard, about halfway down on the right is a tombstone near the cornfield line. The tombstone has a sculpture of a white dog on it. There have been reports of hearing a dog barking near this tombstone when no dog is present.

People that have been in the cemetery at night have reported seeing glowing balls of light moving throughout the cemetery. These balls of light have mostly been seen when using a video camera, but some have been seen with the naked eye.

There has been a sighting of a black ghost cat in the cemetery. If you enter the first driveway going into the cemetery, when traveling east on Alward Road, follow the road into the cemetery until you see a big bush on the right side. A cat was seen in this area near a tombstone.

Two people were walking on the driveway in the cemetery when they saw the cat from a distance, lying near a tombstone. They thought it was odd that a cat would be in the cemetery. But considering the location of the cemetery, they didn't think twice about it. When they passed by the big bush and looked again, the cat was nowhere to be seen.

They didn't see the cat leave, and they had no idea where the cat had gone. When they were walking toward the cat, before it disappeared, they

HAUNTED MICHIGAN GRAVEYARDS

thought it was funny that the cat never acknowledged them. The whole time, the cat never looked up at them or changed its position near the tombstone. They were walking on the driveway, which was gravel, so they made noise as they walked. The cat would have heard them, for sure.

On the east side of the graveyard are a couple of tall trees. Near these trees, people have reported hearing whispers and feeling they were being watched. Of course, there isn't anyone there. You can't make out what is being said, but they are whispers and not the wind.

As mentioned before, there is a small white church in front of the cemetery. Visitors to the cemetery have also seen what appears to be a person looking out the windows toward the cemetery. When investigated, the door to the church is locked, and there is no other way into the building.

Reed Cemetery is a nice little graveyard in the country. Unfortunately, a few years back, some of the tombstones in the cemetery were vandalized. The police make random checks on the cemetery throughout the day and evenings. You will get a trespassing ticket if you are caught in the cemetery after dusk. If you do visit the cemetery, bring a treat in case you happen to encounter the ghost cat. I am sure he will appreciate it!

CHAPTER 5

GENESEE COUNTY

BENDLE CEMETERY, FLUSHING

Bendle Cemetery is a graveyard that according to Google Maps does not rate an address. The graveyard is located on the south side of Beecher Road between North Seymour Road to the east and North Van Vleet Road to the west. The graveyard's hours are from dawn to dusk. There are two entrances to the graveyard off Beecher Road. The graveyard borders a field to the south and houses to the west, east and north. The ages of the tombstones range from the 1800s to current.

If you are going west on Beecher Road and take the first driveway into the cemetery, you will see two trees on your right. There is a tall tombstone for Granger between the trees. In this area, you might encounter a moving cold spot, and on a good day, you might hear voices and have the feeling of being watched.

Follow the road through couple of curves until you are heading west. There will be three tombstones on your right. This is the spot where the apparition of a child has been seen. It is always seen near these three tombstones. It is dressed in early 1900s clothes, and it appears to be a boy. He stands with his head bowed and will simply disappear.

Continue around the curve; you will be heading north, and on your right, you will see a bench that you can sit on. An apparition of a man has been seen sitting on this bench. He has on a suit, and he has been observed just sitting there while looking straight ahead. He does not acknowledge anyone, and he will eventfully fade from sight.

A little ways on your left, you will see a tree that stands all by itself. Orbs have been observed moving around the tree and the tombstones in the area.

Follow the road toward Beecher Road, and as you get to the end of the graveyard, you will see a tombstone on your right that looks like a tree stump with an open book on it. If you stand looking at the book, you get the feeling that something is just not right in this area. You get goosebumps and have the feeling that something is off.

Bendle Cemetery is a well-maintained graveyard. If you stop by for a visit and see either the child or the man sitting on the bench, say "Hi" for me. Thanks.

CALVARY CEMETERY, FLINT

Calvary Cemetery is located in Flint; it is also known as Old Calvary Catholic Cemetery. It has no address, as it doesn't rate one on Google Maps. The graveyard is open from dawn to dusk. It is located on North Ballenger Road, five blocks south of Flushing Road, and is on Chatfield Street, which is the only entrance and exit into and out of the cemetery. The graveyard is surrounded by trees and a ravine to the east, the Flint River to the south, houses to the north and North Ballenger Road to the west.

This graveyard seems "off" as soon enter the driveway into the graveyard. Your first indication that this isn't your run-of-the-mill graveyard is the signs. There are signs attached to poles lining both sides of the driveway leading into the graveyard. The first sign says, "Jesus died for your sins," and the other signs all quote Scripture.

The first impression this graveyard gives is one of neglect. Most if not all of the tombstones are from the 1800s to the early 1900s. Some of the tombstones have fallen over, most likely from age, and some are so weathered that you cannot read them. The grass hasn't been mowed—it's about shin high—and that probably adds to the overall "off" feeling of this graveyard.

Take the first right once you are in the graveyard and follow it until you see a metal sign. This sign states what you can and cannot do in the graveyard. In this area, you feel like either someone is watching you intently or something is standing right behind you. But, of course, when you look

Above: The voices of a man and a woman talking can be heard near here.

Opposite: A woman's sobbing and a child's screams can sometimes be heard around these tombstones.

behind you, there isn't anyone there. The presence doesn't feel threatening by any means: the feeling is more like, "What are you doing here?"

If you continue straight ahead, where the road curves, you will see a tombstone that reads "Lee and Bradley." There have been reports of white balls of light darting in between the tombstones in this area. Some of the balls of light have been observed disappearing in the trees in the area.

There is a monument just to the north of this area. You cannot miss it; it looks like a marble column that you might find in Greece, and the name on it is Walsh. In the area surrounding this unique monument, voices can sometimes be heard. They do not seem to be coming from any one direction; it is like you have surround sound. You cannot make out what is being said, but it sounds like both men and women are talking.

If you look across the road toward the center part of the graveyard, you will see a tombstone with three crosses near it. A woman's sobbing and what sounds like a child screaming can occasionally be heard in this area. Also, a cold spot can be felt in the area between the two crosses, the ones furthest away from the tombstone.

If you follow the road from where the monument that looks like a marble column is and follow the curve, take the first right, and you will see a tall, white tombstone a little ways to the right that says, "Patrick Traynor." Directly in front of this tombstone, right on the road, an apparition of a woman has been seen. She is described as wearing glasses and clothes that would have been popular in the 1950s.

Calvary Cemetery has an overly depressing cloud that seems to hang over the graveyard. I don't know if it is because the graveyard appears to be abandoned or maybe because some of the people laid to rest here find it hard to rest in peace. It is still a cool graveyard to visit. If you cross paths with the apparition of the women, would you say "Hi" for me? Thanks!

CRONK CEMETERY, FLINT

Cronk Cemetery is a pleasant little graveyard. There is no address, but the graveyard is located on Beecher Road between East River Road to the east and Elms Road to the west. The graveyard is open from dawn to dusk. There are two entrances off Beecher Road, and the graveyard is surrounded by a wrought iron fence. The graveyard is surrounded by trees to the west, south and east and Beecher Road to the north.

If you look to your left as soon as you enter the graveyard, you will notice a lone tree at the far east end, along the fence. An apparition of a man has been seen standing near this tree. He has been described as being an older man and dressed like a farmer. He has been seen looking out toward the road.

Directly to the south is an older, vertical tombstone. In this area, there have been reports of hearing a woman sobbing. An orb has also been observed appearing near this area and disappearing once it goes into the trees to the east.

Once in the graveyard, you will see a tall, white tombstone on your right, right next to the road. Directly to the right, people have reported having their shirtsleeves tugged, as if to get their attention. The feeling of being watched has also been reported in this area.

If you go to the woods to the west, you will see a tombstone that has fallen over and is propped up against what I would assume was its base. In this area, there have been reports of hearing a growling sound. The sound comes from the area near the base of the fallen tombstone and not the trees near it. A blue orb has been seen in the woods near this area.

If you drive into the graveyard there is a little hill toward the back of the graveyard. Once you are on top of the little hill, on your left will be a big, old tree. Between the tree and the road, you might see the figure of a man. He has been described as being silver and shimmery. He has no discernible features, and you will not be able to see what clothes he has on. He has been observed walking from the tree, crossing the road and heading toward the trees on the west side, disappearing before he gets to the tree line.

In the southeast corner of the graveyard, you will see three pine trees; one of them has an almost white trunk. It is near these trees that you might hear what sounds like someone saying "hey." It is faint, but it can sometimes be heard. You will also get goosebumps in this area.

Cronk Cemetery is a quaint little graveyard. It has quite a bit of activity, considering its size. If you come across the farmer, try getting his name and get back to me to let me know—I am curious to find out who he is! Thanks!

GLENWOOD CEMETERY, FLINT

Glenwood Cemetery is a historic graveyard located at 2500 West Court Street. The graveyard is open from dawn to dusk. There is a lone entrance off West Court Street. The graveyard is surrounded by trees to the west, West Court Street to the south, the Flint River to the north and a few houses to the east. The graveyard is listed on the National Register of Historic Places by the United States Department of the Interior and is a Michigan Historic Site. According to the plaque placed by the State of Michigan,

> Glenwood Cemetery was established in 1857. It is one of only a few mid-nineteenth-century Michigan cemeteries to feature a rolling landscape with winding roadways. The original cemetery, the western section of the present grounds displays a broad range of historic funerary art. The focal point of the eastern portion, developed in 1925, is a granite Neo-classical-style public mausoleum. Among those buried in Glenwood are Jacob Smith, Flint's first white settler, Governors Henry H. Crapo and Josiah Begole, Lieutenant Governor William M. Fenton, William A. Patterson and James Whiting, carriage and automobile builders, J. Dallas Dort, co-founder of the Durant-Dort Carriage Company and Dort Motor Company, and philanthropist Charles South Mott and Harlow Curtice of the General Motors Corporation.

When you enter the graveyard, the first thing you will notice is the over-the-top mausoleums. One of those belongs to Whiting. Near this area, you might feel cold spots, and in some cases, you will feel like you are being watched. On occasion, you might hear the quiet sobs of a woman.

Cold spots are felt in this area as well as the feeling of being watched.

If you are standing in front of the mausoleum and look to the left and a little behind, you will see a monument for Pierson. It is a tall, rust-colored monument. In this area, you have the feeling of being watched, and on occasion, you might smell cigar smoke even though no one is smoking in the area.

Across the road from the Whiting mausoleum is a tombstone for Dewey. You cannot miss it: the tombstone is a good six feet tall and there are eight tombstones in an arc behind it, two tombstones that are only a foot off the ground in front and a tree line directly behind it. It is in this tree line that there have been sightings of black shadows that will hide behind the trees and then peek out.

If you head to the north a little bit, you will see a monument for Northrop. It is a tall one with a wrought iron fence that forms a circle around it; you cannot miss it. This one is interesting. It does not happen all the time, but sometimes, if you open the gate, go inside the circle and close the gate, you cannot hear any sounds from outside the circle, almost like there is a vacuum in that area. You might be lucky enough to hear the sounds of children laughing in the circle.

In the fenced-in area, you might hear children laughing.

If you follow the tree line to your left, you will come upon an area that has fourteen tombstones in a semicircle and seven more in the center. Orbs have been observed moving in this area, and you will also feel like someone is in the tree line watching you. The air also feels heavy in this area.

When you are ready to leave this historic graveyard, make sure to stay on the roads on the east side of the graveyard. When you are near the front of the graveyard, look to your left, and you will see a mausoleum for Aitken-Fellows. There have been sounds heard from inside, but there is no way that anyone can enter, since it is sealed off.

Glenwood Cemetery is a sprawling graveyard that is steeped with history. It appears that some of the prominent figures who were laid to rest here are still yearning for this world. If you are brave enough to enter the circle at the Northrop monument and experience the vacuum sensation, let me know how you liked it! It is something that you have to experience at least once. It is a very odd but very cool experience.

MONTROSE TOWNSHIP CEMETERY, MONTROSE

Montrose Township Cemetery is a large graveyard located at 9330 Vienna Road, Montrose. The graveyard is bordered by Vienna Road to the south and trees to the west, north and east. Also to the north is an open area that appears to be for future burials. There are five entrances to the graveyard off Vienna Road. The graveyard is open from dawn to dusk.

Take the first entrance into the graveyard, and you will see a cluster of trees to your right. There has been no reported activity here, but the trees are nice looking. A little farther up the road, there is a lone tree on your right just before the curve. There has been activity here. Even though there are no flowers in the general area, there have been reports of people smelling roses.

Follow the curve, and on your left-hand side, you will see a building with a road going around it. I am not sure what purpose the building serves, but it appears to be a church to handle memorial services. I do not think it is a mausoleum, because it does not look like the ones I have seen. If you know what the building is used for, please let me know! The building appears to be a magnet for localized activity. Shadow people have been seen around the building as well as in the trees that surround it. Cold spots have been felt outside, near the rear of the building. The doors to the building are locked, but there have been reports of seeing people moving around inside the building.

Continue straight along the road until the *T*. On your left will be some of the older tombstones, dating to the 1800s. Orbs have been seen weaving in and out of the tombstones, and the sound of people whispering can sometimes be heard just inside the tree line.

Take a left and follow the curve past the building that will be on your left. You will see another area of older tombstones on your left. Near the trees, orbs have been seen and a child's soft crying can sometimes be heard.

Follow the road to your right, and about halfway down on your left will be sculptures of two angels a few feet apart that appear to be kneeling; there is a bench directly behind them. An apparition of a little girl has been seen sitting on the bench. She is wearing a white dress with white socks and black shoes. She has light brown hair and a white ribbon in her hair that is tied in a bow. She just sits there swinging her legs until she vanishes.

Straight ahead at the curve in the road, there is a lone small tree or bush. Directly behind this are tombstones. In this area, voices can be heard, and you may feel you're being watched. Batteries in cameras have been drained after a few minutes in the area even though they were brand new. You leave the area, and the batteries are just fine. An orb has been seen just a few inches off the ground moving away from this area, weaving as it goes.

Montrose Township Cemetery is worth visiting. Except for the road that passes by, the graveyard is fairly quiet. If nothing else, sit on the bench where the little girl has been seen. Maybe she will sit beside you and tell you her name. If you do see her, tell her it is OK for her to move on. If I see her again, I will do the same!

New Calvary Cemetery, Flint

New Calvary Cemetery is a Catholic graveyard located at 4142 Flushing Road. There are two entrances off Flushing Road. The graveyard is surrounded by trees to the west, Flushing Road to the south, open land to the north and I-75 to the east. The graveyard's hours are from dawn to dusk. The graveyard is well maintained, and there is a massive mausoleum located near the northeast part of the graveyard. Pulitzer Prize for Photography recipient William M. Gallagher was laid to rest here.

When you enter the graveyard, take a right, and on your right side you will see a large white sculpture of what looks like Jesus and an angel. If you are standing in front of the sculpture, you will see a cluster of trees behind you and to your left. In this general area, you will feel goosebumps and have the feeling that someone is behind you. When you look, of course, there is no one there.

Continue past the sculpture and take the next left. Immediately on your right side, you will see a couple of large trees. Right behind these trees, people have reported seeing orbs and also hearing their name being called. You may also have the feeling of being watched.

Follow this road till the *T* and take a right. Continue on this road, past the intersection, until the road curves. On your left, you will see a line of trees. The big mausoleum should be across the road to your left. In this area, people have been pushed—not hard, but they received a shove from behind. If that wasn't not enough to cause you concern, there is also a chance that you might be scratched in this area also.

Follow the road around the curve and continue until you see a road to your left. You will see on your right a monument that pays tribute to all the veterans who fought in our nation's wars. Not coincidentally, in this area,

You will get a case of goosebumps and the feeling that you are not alone.

Electronic equipment will fail in this area, and cameras will not work correctly.

you might feel anxiety and sadness. Near the monument, you might hear voices and catch a glimpse of a black shadow that has been seen in this area.

If you follow the road until it curves, you will see another bunch of trees on your right. There have been reports that people have heard a woman quietly sobbing and felt sadness. There also have been reports of an apparition of a child being seen in this area. You will only get a glimpse of the child out of the corner of your eye. As soon as you try to look at it, the child is gone.

Take the left and follow it until you are right behind the huge mausoleum. Just before the curve, you will see a very interesting monument on your left. You cannot miss it. The monument is tall, it has some type of writing on it and it has a gold-looking top, with crosses on top of it. In this area, electronic equipment will fail. Your camera will not take pictures, and if it does, the picture comes out black. It seems that if you ask permission to take a picture, the picture will come out fine.

New Calvary Cemetery seems to have a few spirits that are not at rest. If you plan on visiting this graveyard, you get more than you bargain for. If you happen to experience something that was not listed here, could you please let me know? I will update the list. Thanks in advance!

Pine Run Cemetery, Clio

Pine Run Cemetery is an older graveyard located—according to Google Maps—at 12201 North Dort Highway, Clio. I am not sure why Google Maps lists the address as being on North Dort Highway when it is actually on North Saginaw Road, but it does. There are trees to the west and south. There are houses to the north. To the east is North Saginaw Highway. There is no paved road into the graveyard, but there is a little path that you can drive on and park on, or if you wish, you can always just park on the side of the street. There do not appear to be any newer tombstones here; most of them appear to be from the mid-1800s to early 1900s. The hours are not stated, but I assume they are from dawn to dusk.

Assuming that you park in the graveyard on the little path, as we will be using this as a reference point, the first thing you should see—assuming that you are in the correct graveyard—is a flagpole on your right. Just to the east of the flagpole, you should see a little bush with tombstones. It will have a border of what appear to be bricks around it. There have been cold spots in this area, and electronic equipment will routinely malfunction here.

Again using the path as a reference point, look straight ahead and a little to your left. You will see a big pine tree and tombstones around it. Voices have been recorded in this area, and on one occasion, a voice seemed to be telling a visitor to get out! You also might get the feeling of being watched while in this area.

Again using the path as a reference, look straight and to your right. You will see a tall white tombstone with two smaller white crosses on either side. Here you will sometimes get the feeling of not being wanted in the area. Cold spots have been recorded here. In the tree line to the west, movement can sometimes be seen.

From the path to your right, there will be a tombstone for Lewis with several smaller markers beside it. When there is not much traffic on the road, you can sometimes hear a child laughing, but the sound is coming from this area and not from the road.

To the right of this tombstone, toward the houses to the north, you will see a granite-colored tombstone that is at a precarious angle, looking like it could fall at any time. Right at this tombstone, you might catch a whiff of a pipe being smoked. If you know someone who has ever smoked a pipe, you know the smell well.

From the tilting tombstone toward the road and to the right appear to be some of the older tombstones. Many of these date to the 1800s. There is a white tombstone in this area that has the name Francis A. on it. There has been an apparition of a woman seen kneeling right in front of this tombstone, so I would assume that this is Francis herself. A woman's sobs have also been heard in this area. Again, I am assuming this would be Francis!

Pine Run Cemetery is a smaller and older graveyard that is worth visiting. You might get to smell the pipe being smoked by some unseen presence, and maybe if you are lucky enough, you might even see Francis kneeling by her grave. If you do see Francis, tell her that everything is going to be OK!

Sunset Hills Cemetery, Flint

Sunset Hills Cemetery is a sprawling graveyard located at 4413 Flushing Road. The graveyard is open from dawn to dusk. There are two entrances off Flushing Road and one off Pasadena Road to the north. The graveyard is surrounded by trees to the west, Flushing Road to the south, open land to the north and I-75 to the east. The graveyard is well maintained, and there are some interesting things to see other than tombstones. There are eight sculptures located in the graveyard. They are easy to find; you just need to drive around the graveyard and find them. They are *The Generation Bridge*, *The Gardener, Candice and the Flower Girls, Give Me a Kiss, The Provider, The Flag Raiser, Jesus Christ* and *Crack the Whip*.

Crack the Whip was supposedly commissioned by an elderly gentleman who lost his granddaughter in some kind of accident. The story that has been going around for years is that the sculpture is haunted. There have been reports that you can hear children's laughter around this area. One of the girls in the sculpture lost her sandal; it is lying on the ground a few feet behind the last girl in line. The rumor has it that if your foot can fit in the sandal, you will be the next to die.

If you are facing the sculpture, turn around and you will see a mausoleum up ahead all by itself off the road on the right. It has a little bridge that crosses what looks like a dried-up creek bed. There are stone steps that take you up to the mausoleum. There are trees all around it. The name on it is Northrup. There is a chain with a lock on it, so unfortunately, you cannot enter the mausoleum.

Snap the Whip sculpture. Children's laughter has been heard here.

A black, humanlike form will watch you from the trees near the mausoleum.

Among the trees in the area, there have been sightings of a black, humanlike form that will just stare at you from the trees. If you try to approach it or take a picture, it will vanish quickly. There also have been orbs sighted in the area, darting in and out of the tree line.

If you continue on the road past the mausoleum and stay right at the *Y*, you will come upon a cluster of trees on your left. It is in this area that you might get the feeling of being watched and the feeling that you should not be in this area.

Continue straight until you come to an intersection. Take a right and follow the road until you come to a lone big tree on your right; it will be just after the second curve. This is the area where a woman's cries can be heard. There is also a cold spot that will follow you.

Head toward the northwest section of the graveyard, and you will see the sculpture of Jesus. You cannot miss it, as it is quite tall and it is the only sculpture in the area. It is white, and Jesus's arms are outstretched in front of him. In the area surrounding the sculpture, something does not feel quite right. Once you experience the feeling; you will know what I am talking about.

Sunset Hills Cemetery is a nice graveyard. Overall, the feeling is that spirits here are, for the most part, resting in peace—but not all of them. If you visit the graveyard, make sure and stop at the *Crack the Whip* sculpture. Listen for children's laughter and try and make contact with them. And oh, if you are feeling brave, see if your shoeless foot will fit in the sandal. If it does, please let me know; I am curious. For the record, my foot did not fit on the sandal!

WEST VIENNA CEMETERY, CLIO

West Vienna Cemetery is not as big as some of the other graveyards in this book, but according to Google Maps, it has a range of numbers for its address: 5805–5999 West Wilson Road, Clio. The graveyard has two entrances off West Wilson Road. The graveyard has trees to the west, south and east. There are also a few houses past the trees to the east. West Wilson Road is to the north. Posted hours are from dawn to dusk. Most of the tombstones appear to be from the 1800s to the 1900s.

If you are on West Wilson Road heading west, take the second driveway into the graveyard. If you see the church on West Wilson Road, you have gone too far. As you enter the graveyard, you will see some trees whose branches hang over the road. Continue on a little bit, and you will see some more trees whose branches hang over the road. If you look to your right, you will see a square that is made of either white bricks or stones. Inside this square will be a tall tombstone with three smaller ones behind it. In this square, if you are unlucky enough and the timing is right, you might feel a cold spot and hear someone whispering in your ear, but you cannot make out what is being said.

Continue straight until you see what looks like some type of caretaker's building on your right-hand side. Just past the building on your right will be a small cluster of tombstones. Growling can sometimes be heard coming from the trees directly behind these tombstones. Movement can sometimes be seen in the trees. It has been described as a humanlike figure, but no details can be seen.

If you go straight and take the little roundabout, you will be going in the same direction you just came from. A little way on your right, you will see a tombstone for Jessie; it is tall and weathered. Behind the tombstone is a pine tree. There have been sightings of the apparition of a little girl peeking out from behind this tree like she was playing hide and go seek. If you read the inscription on Jessie's tombstone, you'll see she passed in 1871 at the age of two years and fourteen days. Could this apparition be Jessie playing a game of hide and go seek with you?

Continue going straight a little bit, and you will see on your right, by a tree, a tall tombstone with six smaller markers in front of it. In this general area, there have been reports of orbs moving around the tombstones and the feeling of being watched. Cold spots are often felt in this area.

You will see the same trees with the branches hanging over the road that you saw when you first came into the graveyard. This time, go to the second set of trees whose branches are covering the road. To your right will be a big tree; it is a few feet from the road. In this area, you might feel like something is around your throat, as if you were being choked. There is also a feeling of dread and sorrow in this area.

West Vienna Cemetery is worth visiting just for the chance of seeing Jessie. It is a smaller graveyard and well maintained. If you are lucky enough to see Jessie, and she wants to play a game of hide and go seek, let her win—please!

WOODLAWN MEMORIAL CEMETERY, CLIO

Woodlawn Memorial Cemetery is a big graveyard located at 11163 Clio Road. The graveyard has trees to the north, open fields and trees to the west and trees and a house to the south; to the east is Clio Road with a couple of houses. There are two entrances to the graveyard off Clio Road. The tombstones are mainly from the 1800s and early to mid-1900s, but there are some more recent ones. Posted hours are from dawn to dusk.

If you take the first road into the graveyard, turn right and follow it to just before the curve, on your left will be a tall monument with two markers in front of it and what appear to be five markers behind it. There are white stones that form a square around the monument and markers. In the square, you might feel cold spots, and some have complained of having a headache while in the square. Once they leave the square, the headache goes away.

Go past the curve, and on your right, you will see a few stray tombstones near the trees. Whispers have been heard from just inside the tree line, and a black shadow has been seen moving in the trees. Cold spots have also been felt in this area. Cameras will also malfunction, and it might take a couple of attempts to take a picture.

Follow the road till it curves again. To your left are a couple of trees, and to your right is what appears to be a dirt road or path. Near the trees, people have reported being pushed by unseen hands. If you attempt to walk down the dirt road or path, you might have the pleasure of hearing footsteps like someone is coming up behind you. But when you look, no one is behind you. On occasion, some have reported that when they try to walk down the dirt road or path, after a few feet, they feel like something is stopping them— almost as if some unseen hands are stopping them from going any further.

Follow the road around the perimeter of the graveyard until you are back near Clio Road. Go toward the entrance you came in. Just before that entrance, on your left, there will be three areas where you will see monuments with white bricks forming a square around each monument. Around this cluster of squares, there have been reports of smelling cigar smoke and feelings of being touched. Orbs have also been seen darting around the tombstones in this area.

On occasion, voices have been heard near the trees behind this area to the west. On one occasion, there was a report of someone being scratched on the back in this area. They had their shirt on and felt a burning sensation on their back. After lifting their shirt, three fresh scratches were found on their back; they were red, and welts were still forming.

Woodlawn Memorial Cemetery is worth visiting if you are in the area. Based on the activity here, it would appear that some of the spirits are not happy campers. If you are brave enough to come to this graveyard and end up getting scratched, I don't want to tell you "I told you so," but...

CHAPTER **6**

GRATIOT COUNTY

FULTON CENTER CEMETERY, PERRINTON

Fulton Center Cemetery doesn't have an official address according to Google Maps, but it is located along South Alger Road north of West Ranger Road southeast of Perrinton. The graveyard is surrounded half by fields and half by trees to the east. There are many driveways into the cemetery, and a driveway goes along the graveyard's perimeter. There is a house across the street and a house behind the cemetery to the northeast. Hours are not posted, but I think it would be safe to assume that the cemetery is open from dawn to dusk. The cemetery isn't as wide as it is long.

Behind the Fulton Center Cemetery sign, you will find a couple of trees. Around these trees and the nearby tombstones, there have been reports of being touched. People have reported feeling the sleeves of their shirts being tugged, as if something was trying to get their attention. Also, in this area, there have been reports of hearing whispers and the sensation of being watched.

There is a cluster of trees near the center of the cemetery, near the road, where a picture was taken that appears to show a beam of light coming up from a tombstone. The picture was taken during the day when it was partly cloudy, and that tombstone is the only one that has any kind of light coming from it or reflecting off it.

If you are facing the graveyard with Alger Road to your back, there is a section to your far right that only has a few tombstones. If you go one section to the left, it is in this area that you might encounter the black, shadowlike form. It has been seen walking among the tombstones in this area, but it seems that it doesn't move outside of this section.

Fulton Center Cemetery is a hilly and well-maintained graveyard. If you happen to visit this cemetery and are hoping to have an experience, maybe like having your sleeves pulled, I have one word of advice: be careful what you wish for!

NAME LONG FORGOTTEN, PERRINTON

This graveyard is really small and is surrounded on three sides by trees. There isn't a formal name, and the graveyard doesn't show up on Google Maps; all it shows is a green square but no name. I am sure the graveyard had a name once, but I assume it has been long forgotten. I don't believe the graveyard is still being used, as all the readable tombstones are from the 1800s. Since the graveyard doesn't have a name, I cannot give the exact address. I can tell you, however, that the graveyard is located on the north side of East Ranger Road just before South Alger Road. There is one small driveway off East Ranger Road that goes a couple of feet into the graveyard. The graveyard is southeast of Perrinton. There are no signs indicating the hours the graveyard is open.

Visitors to this small graveyard have heard whispers that sound like they are coming from the trees to the north. There have been photos taken here that depict peculiar streaks of light and mist-like shapes. On numerous occasions, what sounds like a woman moaning has been heard from the tombstones on the far east side of the graveyard. There is a house directly to the north and west of the graveyard. It could be argued that the whispers and moans are coming from these houses, but the sounds appear to be coming from the graveyard.

There are also stories of a small, black shape that has been seen darting between the trees surrounding the cemetery. One of the more popular urban legends that has been going around for years is that of what happened to some teens who were at the graveyard one night years ago.

A group of teens went to the graveyard one night because they were bored. They were joking around and being disrespectful of the people who were laid to rest there. One of the teens felt a burning sensation on his arm. He called his friends over, and one of them shone a flashlight on his arm where he felt the burning. On his arm were three raised scratch marks that were freshly made. Needless to say, the teens left the graveyard immediately.

This graveyard is old and abandoned. It has been forgotten for so long that its name has been forgotten! Just some friendly advice: if you decide to venture to this graveyard, please be respectful. Otherwise, you might find the same scratch marks on your arm.

New Haven Township Cemetery, Sumner

New Haven Township Cemetery is located at 9364 Buchanan Road, Sumner, Michigan 48889. The graveyard is located to the west of Warner Road. The hours are not posted, but I would assume, like many graveyards, it is open from dawn to dusk. There are three driveways in the church. All three go the full length of the graveyard; they all meet a smaller driveway at the south end of the graveyard. Some trees border the graveyard to the east and south. There are open fields to the west. There is one house across the street and to the left. There is a small church in front of the graveyard.

Some visitors to the graveyard have reported seeing handprints on the glass inside the church, even though the church is locked and you can't gain access. There have also been reports of seeing an older woman, in a white dress, looking out the window from inside the church. When visitors go to investigate closer, the church is locked and no one can be seen inside.

If you take the center driveway into the graveyard, in the first section, a little way in, you will see a flagpole on your right, a kind of veterans' memorial. It could be because of the veterans' memorial, but there appears to be more activity in this area. Everything from hearing voices, seeing shadows near tombstones and the general feeling of being watched often occurs in this area of the graveyard.

People have also seen balls of light near the trees on the south side of the graveyard. About halfway into the cemetery, near the driveway by the field, are two big trees. Near these trees, there have been reports of small stones being thrown at people. To this date, none of the stones thrown have hit anyone. It is as if the stones are like warning shots intended to scare people away, a way of saying, "Get out of my area; I don't want you here."

New Haven Township Cemetery is well maintained and a nice place to visit during the fall because of all the trees changing color. If you are in the area and decide to stop in for a visit, and you happen to see the older woman in the church, please see if you can get her name; we all want to know who she is! Thanks in advance.

PAYNE CEMETERY, PERRINTON

Payne Cemetery doesn't have an official address, but it is located on South Ely Highway just north of County Line Road. Even though Google lists the cemetery as being in Perrinton, the cemetery is in fact in Fulton Township. The cemetery is in the countryside, surrounded by trees to the north, east and south and South Ely Highway to the west. The older section and mausoleum are in the south part of the cemetery, and the newer section and open plots are in the north section. Three driveways lead into the cemetery. The graveyard's hours are from dawn to dusk. The dates on the tombstones range from the 1800s to current.

Payne Cemetery is a historic site, according to a sign in the cemetery, but the reason for this claim is not listed on the sign. After a quick search online, I couldn't find why the cemetery is a historic site.

There have been numerous stories of strange events happening in the cemetery, mainly in the evening, after the sun has gone down. One of the main stories is about the big tombstone of a man sitting in a chair, facing the road. The tombstone in question is a few rows away from the road and cannot be missed; the name on the tombstone is Elsworth. This is a story that I heard growing up. The man wanted to be buried near the road, and he designed the tombstone himself. He reportedly said he wanted to be buried near the road so that he could continue to watch the world go by after he passed. But according to some of the stories being told, he wasn't content to just sit and watch.

I have heard stories about this tombstone for as long as I can remember. People have reportedly seen the statue of the man get out of his chair and move around his tombstone. Others have seen him move in his chair but not move around on the ground.

There is a tombstone a few feet north of the mausoleum, to the left of the driveway, where many people have felt cold spots even on hot summer days. Around this tombstone, people have captured ectoplasmic mist in pictures.

Between the newer and older sections, there have been reports of hearing laughter, hearing a man speaking but being unable to make out what is being said and the feeling of being watched.

If you park on the driveway right in front of the mausoleum and a few feet toward the road, you might hear phantom footsteps. According to one report, two visitors to the cemetery parked in that spot with the front of their vehicle facing the road. One of them stayed in the vehicle while the other one was walking in the cemetery. It was fall, and there were dead

A story has it that the man on the monument comes to life and moves around the graveyard.

Go into the mausoleum and close the doors; footsteps have been heard in here.

leaves on the ground, the kind where if you walk on them, they crunch under your feet.

The person who remained in the vehicle had the windows down and heard leaves crunching between the vehicle and the mausoleum, as if someone was walking toward the vehicle. When they got out and looked behind them, there wasn't anyone there, but they could still hear the footsteps coming toward them. The sound of the leaves crunching stopped a few feet from the vehicle.

There have also been reports of footsteps being heard from inside the mausoleum. The door to enter the mausoleum is unlocked, and you can go in if you are brave enough. The floor of the mausoleum is tiled, and you can hear your footsteps as you walk. There are vaults on both sides.

The story goes that if you go into the mausoleum and close the door, you will immediately feel like you are being watched. If you walk toward the back of the mausoleum and stop a few feet from the wall, you will hear three more footsteps on the tile floors even though you have stopped!

Payne Cemetery is a nice graveyard to visit if you have a free afternoon. If you decide to visit the cemetery and just happen to see a statue of a man walking around, tell him "Hi" for me. You have to go inside the mausoleum at night, turn off your lights and close the door. Walk toward the back of the mausoleum, let me know if you hear the extra footsteps behind you!

CHAPTER 7

INGHAM COUNTY

MOUNT HOPE CEMETERY, LANSING

Mount Hope Cemetery is located at 1800 East Mount Hope Avenue in Lansing. This graveyard is open from dawn to dusk. It is huge! East Mount Hope Avenue borders the graveyard to the north, North Aurelius Road to the east and Sycamore Creek to the west; houses are to the south of the graveyard. There is a Michigan Historical Marker in the graveyard.

The front of the marker reads:

> *Mount Hope Cemetery opened as Lansing's new city cemetery in June 1874 on what was formerly the John Miller Farm. Between 1874 and 1881 the city vacated the Lansing City Cemetery, located on the site of what would become Oak Park, and moved roughly one thousand graves to Mount Hope. Frederick W. Higgins, superintendent of Detroit's Woodmere Cemetery, planned the drives, and Henry Lee Bancroft, Lansing cemetery superintendent and director of parks and recreation from 1914 to 1957, developed the landscape over many years. The rolling terrain, curving drives, and variety and profusion of monuments reflect cemetery concepts of the mid nineteenth century. A large obelisk, the city's Civil War soldier's monument was dedicated in 1878 on one of the highest points in the cemetery.*

The back of the marker reads:

Mount Hope Cemetery contains the remains of some of the capital city's most prominent citizens, as well as some of the least privileged. Industrialists such as Ransom Eli Olds, pioneer botanist Dr. William J. Beal, and two-time Medal of Honor winner and surgeon Dr. George Ranney are buried here as well as state officials and university presidents. A section platted in 1874 for the State Reform School (later the Boys Vocational School) holds the remains of sixty-one boys who died between roughly 1860 and 1933. In addition, the remains of Lieutenant Luther Baker, who led the effort to capture John Wilkes Booth, the assassin of President Abraham Lincoln, are here, as well as those of Lucy Karney, a formerly enslaved African American who died in 1879 at the age of 117.

Some of the victims of the Bath school bombing are laid to rest here. The marker states that Ransom Eli Olds, the founder of the Oldsmobile motor company, is laid to rest here. There is also a mausoleum for the Price family. Lawrence Price was a Civil War veteran and politician. There are no fewer

R.E. Olds mausoleum. He was the founder of the Oldsmobile car company.

A woman in white has been seen moving in this area.

than four U.S. congressmen laid to rest here. They are Claude Ernest Cady, Grant Martin Hudson, Patrick Henry Kelley and John Wesley Longyear.

I like to give you detailed directions to places where you might encounter the paranormal, but this graveyard has so many roads in the graveyard itself that it would be too confusing to do so. I think you, the reader, would be better off just going to this graveyard and taking your time exploring it. There are so many cool monuments and famous people buried here! But…

Do find the mausoleum for Lawrence Price; it is in an area where there are roads on each side, and it is closer to Aurelius Road to the east. There are also large bushes on either side of the entrance to the mausoleum, which faces east.

If you face the front of the entrance and go around the left side, you will find a marker for Ellen. It is very possible that in this area, you will feel an overwhelming sense of sadness. You may also feel a sense of confusion. You cannot get into the mausoleum, but if you take a picture of the inside through the glass, you might get an orb or two.

Around the Sycamore Creek side of the graveyard, you will see an obelisk for Clark. It is in this area that you might encounter the woman in white.

She has been seen walking—make that floating—near the obelisk. She is dressed in white with jet-black hair. She is only seen for a few minutes and then slowly disappears.

Near the obelisk for the Civil War veterans' monument, there have been reports of voices being heard. It is a full-on conversation between two or more people. You cannot make out what is being said, but there is a conversation going on.

Mount Hope Cemetery has quite a bit of history to it. If you are in the mood for exploring a very cool graveyard, I would recommend coming here. There are many famous people laid to rest here, and there is a good chance you just might encounter their spirits. If you encounter the spirit of a veteran, like always, thank them for their service. If you encounter the spirit of Ransom Eli Olds, you might not want to tell him that the company he founded went out of business.

SAINT JOSEPH CEMETERY, LANSING

Saint Joseph Cemetery is located at 2520 West Willow Street in Lansing. This graveyard is open from dawn to dusk. The Grand River borders the graveyard to the north. There is a commercial complex to the east and houses to the west. Willow Street borders the graveyard to the south.

Enter the graveyard off Willow Street and take a right. Follow the road past the office and continue straight until you come to a Y in the road. To your left, people have seen a group of three or four people who are just walking in the graveyard. They appear to be a little hazy, and they are transparent. They don't acknowledge anyone near them, and if you follow them, they dart behind the big tree and disappear.

Take the right road at the Y and follow it down to where the road curves. To your left, there has been a sighting of three people dancing around the tombstones. Like the people walking in the graveyard, they never acknowledge anyone in the area. They have been seen on numerous occasions. They are always in this area, but they do not seem to have a favorite tombstone, as they have been seen dancing around different tombstones.

Continue on this road till a road intersects yours from the left. There will be a big tree standing at the point where the two roads meet. This is the area where you might hear what sounds like someone crying or sobbing. If you look around, nothing and no one can be seen making this noise.

If you continue straight until the road curves, you will see a little circular drive on your right. If you look to your right, you will see two trees. It is at these trees that people have seen a ball of light. It zigzags around the trees and disappears in the distance. There also have been reports of hearing a noise that sounds something like two pieces of wood being hit against each other.

Saint Joseph Cemetery is a sprawling graveyard in the city. If you are brave enough to venture to this graveyard, keep an eye out for either the people dancing around the tombstones or the people walking the graveyard. If you happen to come across them, try and see who they are. I would be interested in their names and where they are walking to.

CHAPTER 8
IONIA COUNTY

DANBY CEMETERY, SUNFIELD

Danby Cemetery, like some of the other graveyards in this book, doesn't have an actual address, but it is located on Charlotte Highway north of East Tupper Lake Road. The graveyard is located at a curve in the road on a little hill. The graveyard is surrounded by trees to the west, open fields to the south and Charlotte Highway to the north and east. The older section has tombstones dating from the early 1800s to the mid-1900s. As you drive into the cemetery, the new section is on your left and the older section is on your right. There is a tree line near the older section. The newer section also has tombstones from the mid-1900s to the present. The cemetery is open from dawn to dusk.

There is a story that has been going around the area for years about a ghost child seen crossing the road in front of the cemetery. My wife has a friend who has seen her. The friend was driving a coworker home from work one night, and as he rounded the curve in front of the graveyard, they saw a girl wearing a white dress crossing the road in front of them. She was heading away from the graveyard. He said that she looked real and was a little spooked when he saw her.

Supposedly there was once a house across the road from the cemetery. It burned down years ago, and a little girl died in the fire. The little girl is said to be buried in the graveyard. Is the little girl seen crossing the road the little girl that supposedly died in the fire? If so, why is she crossing the road? Is she going back to where the house once stood or going into the graveyard trying to find her body?

The little girl's name is Martha, according to the stories. Are the little girl who crosses the road and Martha one and the same? There is a tombstone in the older section that is for Martha. Could this be the little girl's final resting place? There was a picture taken a few

Could this be Martha's tombstone?

years back in the older section of the cemetery, not too far from Martha's tombstone. In the picture, you can make out what appears to be the apparition of a little girl walking near a tree. Ironically, the little girl is walking toward the road in front of the cemetery. Could this be Martha?

Danby Cemetery is a nice little graveyard that rates a visit. If you are driving on the road in front of the cemetery, either by day or night, and happen to see a little girl crossing the road, you might have been lucky enough to see Martha. She means you no harm, and it doesn't mean you will die soon or anything like that. She is just doing something unknown that only she understands.

CHAPTER 9
JACKSON COUNTY

OAKWOOD CEMETERY, JACKSON

You never know what you will encounter when doing research for a book. The wife and I were in Jackson trying to find Little Mary's tombstone in Hillcrest Memorial Park. We drove around the graveyard for an hour trying to find her tombstone. We couldn't find it, so we decided to ask someone where it was.

I found a couple of graveyard workers. They knew what I was referring to but said that I couldn't get to her tombstone from the graveyard. One of the workers told me that the section where Mary is buried was called Oakwood Cemetery, but that graveyard doesn't exist any longer. They said people have been vandalizing the tombstone for years and access from the graveyard is restricted. The two workers said they, unfortunately, couldn't tell me exactly how to get to the tombstone due to policy. They did, however, in a roundabout way, tell me how to find the tombstone if I was so inclined.

I tried to find the tombstone with their directions but have not found it yet. I will be making a return trip and will try again to find Mary's tombstone. When we got home, I used Google Maps and have a pretty good idea of where the tombstone is now.

However, while trying to find Mary's tombstone, I did have an encounter in the old Oakwood Cemetery that I think is worth mentioning here. It was unexpected and exhilarating at the same time.

To get to the old Oakwood Cemetery, leave Hillcrest Memorial Park, turn right on North Elm Avenue and then turn right on Blake Road. On the right-hand side, about half a mile down Blake Road, you will see a little half-circle dirt area. Park here and follow the trail that leads into the woods. I won't lie: the old cemetery is about a half-mile walk on trails and through trees. Stay on the paths, and when there is an option, stay left. You will soon get to the first tombstone; you will be in the middle of the woods.

It is at the first set of tombstones where I had my encounter. I had stopped to take some pictures of the first set of tombstones. There were two on the left and two on the right. After I took a picture of the tombstones on the left, I looked up and saw a black form crossing the path, from left to right. It was heading away from me, not more than twenty feet in front of me. It was the shape and size of a man.

The black form was off the path moving through the trees; it didn't make a sound. I started to follow it. I stayed on the path, but I had the black form in my sights the whole time. I followed it until it came to a cluster of tombstones on this small hill. There were two taller tombstones on top

This is the area where the black form was first seen.

On top of the hill is where the black form "melted" into the ground.

of this hill, and as the black form went between these two tombstones, it vanished. It was as if it just melted into the ground.

I took a few pictures of those two tombstones after the fact. In hindsight, I should have taken pictures of the black form while I was following it. But I was too intent on keeping it in sight and trying not to trip over anything on the path.

I took a few more pictures and headed back to the car. I don't know who or what the black form was. I don't know why it was on the path, and I don't know why I was allowed to see it. It was a very interesting experience, though. I plan on going back to the woods to see if there are any other tombstones that I missed the first time. And, of course, to hopefully see the black form again. This time, I promise to get its picture!

Oakwood Cemetery has long been forgotten. There are only a few tombstones remaining, and they are scattered around the area. If you feel adventurous, you have to go to the old Oakwood Cemetery. Just stay on the trails, and you will be fine. Hopefully, you will encounter the black form for yourself. If you do, say "Hi" for me, if you would. Thank you!

Reynolds Cemetery, Jackson

Reynolds Cemetery (a.k.a Crouch Cemetery) is located at 6060 Horton Road, Jackson, Michigan. The graveyard is extremely small and surrounded by a chain-link fence. There is a church to the south, trees to the west, a house directly to the north and to the east, Reynolds Road runs directly beside the graveyard. The posted hours are from eight o'clock in the morning to dusk. You wouldn't think that a graveyard this small could be a hot spot for paranormal activity, but it appears that it is.

You'll need to read about Woodland Cemetery, the cemetery after this one, to learn about the Crouch murders that happened in 1883. The father, Jacob Crouch, is buried here at Reynolds Cemetery. I am not sure which grave is his, since a lot of the tombstones are so faded with age that they are hard to read.

Some stories about this graveyard have been around since the 1980s. The most common story is that on the anniversary of the murders, November 21, close to midnight, the spirit of Jacob's daughter Eunice White makes the trek from her final resting place in Woodland Cemetery to see her father in Reynolds Cemetery. Her spirit is most commonly seen as a white mist. It is said that once Eunice's spirit gets to her father's tombstone it simply disappears.

As you can imagine, many paranormal investigators descend on this graveyard on November 21 to try and get a glimpse of Eunice if she makes her appearance. Because of this, the local police patrol the area heavily on this day, and they will ask you to leave if you are on the graveyard grounds. If you are caught there after hours, you will be given a citation for trespassing.

I would not recommend parking on the street, as it does get quite busy at times. You can park in the church parking lot, but there is a sign posted stating that any unauthorized vehicles will be towed at the owner's expense. But I think you would be OK if you just parked there for a short time.

The appearance of Eunice White isn't the only thing paranormal happening at this graveyard. There have been reports of people seeing white balls of light weaving through the trees on the west side of the graveyard. People have also reported being in the graveyard and seeing people looking at them from inside the church when the church is indeed empty.

Reynolds Cemetery is a graveyard that is old but has some history to it. If you intend to visit on November 21 to try and get a glimpse of Eunice White as she makes an appearance, just be mindful of the usual heavy police presence and large gathering of other paranormal enthusiasts. If you do go, and Eunice White makes an appearance and you get the chance, could you do me a favor? Could you ask her who did it and let me know what she said? I would be interested to know the answer! Thanks in advance!

WOODLAND CEMETERY, JACKSON

Woodland Cemetery is located at 2615 Francis Street, Jackson, Michigan. There are no signs posted, but I assume the hours the cemetery is open is from dawn to dusk. The graveyard is surrounded by houses on three sides and by Saint John Catholic Cemetery to the east. There is one driveway off Francis Street, and you also can get into the graveyard from Saint John Catholic Cemetery.

There are a couple of spots in the graveyard that don't feel quite right. And there are a couple of people laid to rest here who have something to do with something that happens at another cemetery. First, let us cover the areas that might be paranormal in nature.

When you enter the graveyard from Francis Street, stay to the right. Continue until you can turn right and then continue straight. Keep going straight until you come to the *T* and then turn right. Continue straight until you see a cool mausoleum for a Dr. W.H. Palmer. On this stretch of road, a little before the mausoleum, you might feel like someone is following you if you're walking, or if you are driving a vehicle, you will feel like something is in there with you. The feeling is pretty strong. If you do feel like something is with you, I would strongly recommend that you smudge yourself and your vehicle before you go home. Otherwise, you might be taking a guest home with you!

Leave Dr. Palmer and head straight. When you can, take a left. Continue straight and take the second right. Follow this road till the next *T*. In front of you is a huge mausoleum called Woodland Abbey. There is a semicircular driveway in front of it; park there. When I was there, it was locked, so I couldn't go inside.

If you look through the front door glass, you will have the sensation that someone is watching you from inside. The feeling won't come from one area; you get the feeling that many are looking at you.

If you leave Woodland Abbey and take a right, continue straight until the driveway curves left. Continue a little bit, then take a left and stop. If you look to your left, you will see a whole section of small, unmarked tombstones.

Dr. W.H. Palmer's mausoleum. There is a presence just up the road from here.

It looks like either a paupers' section or something belonging to a hospital. All the tombstones are no more than a few feet tall and resemble each other. They all have numbers on them, with no other identifying information—except one. One of the tombstones lays flat, and it has this written on it:

> *Our 10952*
> *Died*
> *Aug 2,*
> *1919*

This whole section feels a little off, but the marker for 10952 is where you will feel extreme sadness. If you stand in front of it, you will feel sadness, almost to the point that you will start crying. I searched on Google to try and find the history of this section, but I couldn't find anything. There have to be records of some sort someplace; I will keep looking. This section intrigues me.

Now, let's get to the connection with Reynolds Cemetery in Jackson. If you Google "Crouch murders," you will get many results. In a nutshell, back

Monument to the Whites, victims of an unsolved murder.

on November 21, 1883, four people were murdered in a house in Spring Arbor Township. To this day, the crime is unsolved. The people killed that day were Jacob Crouch; his daughter Eunice White; her husband, Henry; and a cattle buyer named Moses Polley.

85

You can find the White family monument when you first enter the graveyard off Francis Street; it will be right in front of you, near the trees. It is tall and white, and it has a cross on top. The tombstones of Eunice and Henry can be found right in front of the White family monument. You can't miss them: Eunice is on the left and Henry on the right, and they have the word *assassinated* written on their tombstones. The White family monument has what looks like a poem inscribed on it, but it is hard to read and you can't make out what the poem says.

Woodland Cemetery is a large graveyard with some very interesting mausoleums and older tombstones. Read the previous chapter to see what Eunice White has to do with another graveyard. If you happen to visit this cemetery, I would strongly recommend that you smudge yourself before leaving to prevent any unwanted guests from following you home.

CHAPTER 10
MONTCALM COUNTY

CARSON CITY CEMETERY, CARSON CITY

Carson City Cemetery doesn't have an actual address, but it is located at the end of North Williams Street in Carson City. There are two graveyards at the end of this street. There is a Catholic cemetery on the right, and Carson City cemetery is on the left. The graveyard is surrounded by trees to the west and north, some kind of industrial buildings to the south and North Williams Street to the east. There is one driveway into the graveyard, and other driveways branch out from the main one. There is also a nice veterans' memorial as soon as you enter the graveyard on the right-hand side. The graveyard is open from eight o'clock in the morning to dusk.

Like most of the other graveyards in this book, there isn't anyone "famous" laid to rest here. There is a victim of the Bath School bombing, though. There does seem to be a fairly good-sized veterans' section. There are a couple of small mausoleums in the graveyard. There are also a few of the really old, ornate tombstones that were popular in the late 1800s and early 1900s.

Maybe because of the large number of veterans buried here, there have been a large number of occurrences around the veterans' memorial; people have reported seeing shadows, hearing voices and feeling as though they were being watched.

The veteran's memorial where shadows have been seen and voices heard.

The famous Little North Shade Block; strange pictures have been taken in this area.

There is a section at the far west side of the cemetery dubbed "Little North Shade Block." This is a small section of tombstones. I am not sure why this section is called what it is. I tried to find a reason using Google but came up empty. There is no other area in the graveyard that has its own section or block.

In the block, you might hear voices coming from the area near the trees, experience cold spots and see the so-called woman in white walking around. Some pictures taken in this area have shown strange white mist and vortices that were not seen with the naked eye. A few round white orbs have also been photographed in this area.

Carson City Cemetery is a good-sized graveyard. It would be worth taking the time to walk among the tombstones and see what you can experience. If you go to this graveyard and happen to see the woman in white roaming around the "block," could you please ask her what "Little North Shade Block" means? Then could you please let me know? I am curious to know what that means. Thanks.

CHAPTER 11
SAGINAW COUNTY

RIDGE ROAD CEMETERY, OAKLEY

Ridge Road Cemetery is a smaller graveyard that is located at 17000 West Ridge Road. There are two entrances to the graveyard. The graveyard is surrounded by trees to the south, a couple of houses to the west, open fields to the east and West Ridge Road to the north. The tombstones seem to range from the 1800s to the present. The hours are from dawn to dusk.

If you are heading east, you will want to take the first entrance. Follow the curve, and on your right, there is the first cluster of tombstones. If you go south and get off the graveyard property, you will see a pond. The pond is visible from the graveyard. The reason I mention the pond is that some people have reported hearing what sounds like people in it. The sound of splashing has been heard, but when you look, there is not anyone in the pond.

A little way on your left, you will see a bush. It will be the only bush in the general area. There is a white tombstone that has "Lida" on it. There is what looks like a log that is part of the tombstone, and the letters that make up the name look like pieces of wood also. Around this tombstone, EVPs have been recorded that sound like a little child. You cannot tell what is being said, however. You also get the feeling that you are being watched.

Up ahead, you will see an intersection. On your right, there are a couple of trees and some tombstones. In this area, there have been reports of orbs moving and then heading into the trees. There have also been cold spots and the familiar "being watched" feeling.

Past the intersection and on your left in the middle of this section, you will see a tall, white tombstone for Walter. Near the tombstone, you might feel dread or sadness. A woman's cries have been heard on occasion in this area. EVPs also have been recorded here.

Continue straight until you see a lone tree on the right side of the road, just before you get to the road off the graveyard property. There are a few tombstones in the area of the tree. There have been sightings of orbs that start from this area; they cross the road into the center part of the graveyard and then disappear. In this area, people have taken pictures, and in the pictures, there have been ectoplasmic, mist-like images. No one was smoking, and it was not cold enough for it to be one's breath.

Ridge Road Cemetery is a nice graveyard and appears to be well maintained. If you visit, you just might hear the sounds of people splashing coming from the pond that is just off the graveyard property. But I bet if you do hear the splashing and you look, there won't be anyone there.

SAINT MICHAEL'S CEMETERY, OAKLEY

Saint Michael's Cemetery is a small graveyard that is located at 401–499 Root Street. There isn't a road into the graveyard, but there is an area in front of the street where you can park. The graveyard has Root Street to the west, some kind of industrial buildings to the north and woods to the south and east. The graveyard is deceiving from the road; it goes back farther than you can see. The tombstones are from the 1800s to the 1900s. There don't seem to be any new burials. The hours are from dawn to dusk.

There is a bell mounted near the sign in the front of the graveyard and a statue of Saint Michael on the right side near the front. Also near the front of the graveyard is a monument that has a small version of the Pietà with a cross behind it. Near this monument, orbs have been seen among the tombstones. Cold spots have also been felt in this area.

Behind the Pietà statue, you will find a tombstone that is in the shape of a cross; it is brown, and the left arm of the cross has broken off. In this area, you might hear the quiet sobbing of a woman, and EVPs have been recorded in the area, but you can't make out what is being said.

There is a tombstone about halfway back that has a cross on it. Near this tombstone, you might see the orb that has been observed in this area. It has been seen floating among the tombstones and disappearing toward the

A smaller version of the Pietà. Cold spots have been felt in this area.

back of the graveyard. Directly in front of this tombstone, you will see a tall monument with two other tombstones to the left. There is also a bush in the area for easy identification. Between these tombstones, there has been a sighting of the apparition of a nun. She is dressed in all black and is looking down. She has been seen walking among these three tombstones.

To the right, near the tree line, there is another tombstone with a cross on it. Ironically, this is the tombstone of a nun. I don't know if this is the same nun who has been seen just a few feet away to the left. In the trees to the south of the nun's tombstone, there have been reports of what sound like tree knockings. They are always heard in threes. I know that tree knockings have been attributed to Bigfoot, but they have also been connected to the paranormal. Three knocks are sometimes associated with evil spirits, and they are used to mock or insult the Holy Trinity: the Father, the Son and the Holy Ghost. The fact that the knocking sounds just happen to be heard in the area of the nun's tombstone can't be a coincidence!

Saint Michael's Cemetery is a Catholic graveyard and appears to be well maintained. It might be wise to say a little prayer for protection before you enter this graveyard. Hopefully, you will catch a glimpse of the nun while she is walking among those tombstones. If you happen to hear the three tree

An apparition of a nun has been seen in this area, and knocks from the trees have been heard.

knocks coming from the woods near the nun's tombstone, try doing three tree knocks yourself. If you hear three tree knocks in response, then we know we have a Bigfoot sighting and it isn't anything paranormal. At least we would know for sure!

CHAPTER 12
SHIAWASSEE COUNTY

ALTON CEMETERY, OWOSSO

Alton Cemetery is a nice little graveyard located at 1999–1001 Pittsburg Road. The graveyard has trees to the west, Pittsburg Road to the south, trees to the north and open fields to the east. There are two entrances to the graveyard off Pittsburg Road. There are quite a few tombstones from the 1800s and only a few from the 1900s. The hours are from dawn to dusk.

If you are heading east on Pittsburg Road, take the first entrance. There will be a lone tombstone on your left in front of the trees. This is the area where you might feel cold spots and the ever-present feeling of being watched, and you might hear movement in the trees when there is no one to be seen.

Directly to the east, across the road, you will see a cluster of tombstones. There are a couple that you are looking for. There should be a tall tombstone that says, "Fenner." It will be the tallest tombstone in that area. An apparition of what looks like a Civil War soldier—without the musket—has been seen by the Fenner tombstone. He has been described as in his twenties, with brown hair. Gunpowder has sometimes been smelled in the area also. You cannot take a picture in this area without first asking for permission.

If you go straight on the road, you will see a big shrub on your left-hand side. There will be some tombstones behind it. In this area, people have heard a woman sobbing, seen orbs moving in the trees and have experienced the feeling of helplessness.

Ahead you will see a building on the left. Walk toward the back of the northwest corner. There you will see one lone tombstone. In this general area, EVPs have been recorded of a woman. She appears to be a friendly spirit, because it sounds like she is saying "Hi"! Also in this area, EMF meters have recorded spikes when there is not an obvious source.

Follow the curve, and you will see three tombstones in a row; they will be on your right. In this area, there have been sightings of a ghost cat. The cat is black and has been seen walking from these three tombstones toward the three to the west. It has also been seen walking back and forth. It does not acknowledge anything in the area. It will be walking and then gradually disappear.

As you get closer to Pittsburg Road, there will be a line of seven tombstones in a row on your right. Orbs have been seen weaving in and out of the tombstones in this area. Unexplained streaks of light have been seen in pictures taken in the area, when no light was seen when the picture was taken. The Civil War soldier has been also seen in this area, looking out toward the open field to the east. You may feel you are being watched; it could be the spirit of the Civil War soldier that is causing that feeling.

I have used trigger objects in the past with success. If you are not aware of what these are, they are items that might elicit a reply from a spirit. For example, you might put a toy or two where a child spirit might be present and then leave the area, and the toys might be moved when you come back.

I am going to send you on another scavenger hunt. Somewhere in this graveyard is a marker for a child who passed away at one year old. The last name is Baker. The only clue I will give you is that his maker rests flat on the ground. Place a small ball near his marker and leave the area. Come back in about half an hour and see if the ball has moved.

Alton Cemetery is an older, smaller graveyard that is worth a visit. Just going by the tombstones alone, there is a lot of history here. As a bonus, you might catch a glimpse of the resident ghost cat. You might want to bring a trigger object, like a bag full of catnip, and see if you get any reaction from the ghost cat. If you visit and happen to see the Civil War soldier, make sure you thank him for his service. Did the ball move for you, too?

CUMMIN CEMETERY, LENNON

Cummin Cemetery is an abandoned cemetery located at 3633 North New Lothrop Road. I find it kind of funny that this abandoned graveyard has an actual address when some of the other graveyards that are still in use do not. The graveyard is small and overgrown with grass and weeds. There is no driveway into it. You can park across the street at the entrance to a field. There is a small depression near the road that runs the length of the graveyard. There is a little bridge-like structure that you can cross to get into the graveyard. The graveyard is surrounded by trees and swampland to the west, north and south. To the east is North New Lothrop Road. Hours are not posted, but I can say with some confidence that you can be there whenever you wish and no one will say anything to you.

According to the sign just inside the graveyard, Cummin Cemetery was founded in 1850. Also, according to the sign, there are at least fifty people buried here. There are only a handful of visible tombstones or markers, suggesting that either the majority of them are missing or nature has reclaimed them. The dates that people were buried here range from 1851,

Some of the tombstones in the forgotten graveyard.

the first, to 1902, the latest. The graveyard is overgrown, so take precautions against ticks, since they can carry pathogens that cause disease.

This graveyard has a history of messing with audio equipment. As soon as you enter the graveyard, you can hear an audible moaning or low humming sound. However, when you try to record it on video, the video part works fine, but you have no audio! The sound is coming from the trees directly to the north of the graveyard property. If you look in that area, however, there is nothing but trees and swampland. There is not a house in sight. There is no logical reason or cause for the sound.

Two different phones were tested outside the graveyard. Video was taken and played back before entering the graveyard. On both phones, video and audio worked as they should. Once inside the graveyard, however, the video worked as it should, but no audio was recorded.

Cummin Cemetery is an abandoned graveyard, and it is sad that the people laid to rest here have no family who can come and see them and are largely forgotten. If you visit and are able to record any kind of audio in the graveyard, please let me know how you did it. Thanks.

ELMWOOD CEMETERY, NEW LOTHROP

Elmwood Cemetery is a sprawling graveyard that is on both sides of the road. The graveyard is located at 7490 Saginaw Street. There are two entrances to the section on the west side of the road and three entrances to the section on the east side. The section on the west side is surrounded to the west, north and south by farmland and Saginaw Street to the east. The section to the east has Saginaw Street to the west and trees to the south, north and east. The graveyard is open from dawn to dusk.

Let us start with the section to the west. This appears to be the newer section, since the tombstones appear to be newer. Take the first entrance and continue until it curves. The first three tombstones have had activity near them. A woman's quiet sobbing has been heard here and EVPs recorded that sound like someone is asking for help.

Look ahead at the next curve and you will see a lone tree. There have been reports of a doglike creature seen near the tree and the surrounding area. The creature has been observed going from the graveyard into the tree line a little to the north. It has also been observed coming back into the graveyard, where it promptly disappears.

Head back to Saginaw Street and turn right, then take the first entrance into the other section of the graveyard. This section is much bigger and has some tombstones that date from the 1800s to the present.

If you follow the road to where it curves, there has been some reported activity here. Most of the activity occurs in the trees right before the curve on the right-hand side. Some of the reported activities are hearing what sounds like a dog growling, movement in the trees when nothing can be seen and the intense feeling of being watched.

Go to the next intersection and look down the road. You will see trees with branches hanging over the road. The first set of trees is where you might encounter the apparition of what appears to be a man. It is hard to tell, since you can only see it from a distance. Whenever you try and get a closer look, it disappears. Orbs also have been seen in this area weaving in and out of the trees.

Continue to the north, and you are in the northern section of the graveyard. About halfway in this section, going toward Saginaw Street, if you are lucky enough, you will feel a temperature drop and your head will start to hurt because the surrounding air pressure drops. If you move a few feet in any direction, your head will stop hurting and the temperature will return to normal.

Elmwood Cemetery is a big graveyard that covers a large area, but it is worth spending time here just walking around and seeing what you can feel. If you encounter the apparition, maybe of a man, get a name if you can, and let me know who it is. Thanks in advance.

FREMONT CEMETERY, BANCROFT

Fremont Cemetery is a large graveyard. As big as it is, however, Google Maps deems that it does not rate an actual address. The graveyard is located on Grand River Road south of I-69 and north of Lemon Road. Interestingly enough, there is another graveyard across the street, and that one is called North Fremont Cemetery! But to make things a little simpler, we will treat these graveyards as one big one. I will refer to them as the south and north sections, with North Fremont cemetery being the north section. The south section seems to be the older section; most of the tombstones are from the 1800s. The north section seems to be the more current one for burials. The south section has four entrances off Grand River Road, while the north section has two. The south section has open fields to the west and south and Grand River Road to the north and east. The north section has a library to the west, Grand River Road to the south and trees to the north and east. The hours for both sections are from dawn to dusk.

Coming from I-69, take the first entrance into the south section. Halfway on the right-hand side, in the area of the third row of tombstones, cold spots have been felt and orbs have been seen weaving in and out of the tombstones. A picture was taken a few years ago in this area that showed a person next to a tombstone who had his arm resting on top of it. But no one was there when the picture was taken.

Take the next left and follow the road past the second left. This is the biggest part of the south section. On your left and somewhere in the middle of this area, there will be a tall obelisk with the name Simonson on it. There will be five tombstones in front of it. In this section, orbs have been seen moving about. People have also had the feeling of being watched and feelings of sorrow in this area.

Continue straight until the road turns into a Y. Take the left, and in front of you will be a big tree. Under the tree, people have been scratched, usually on the back—again, deep enough to draw blood and raise a welt! Not surprisingly, the feeling of not being wanted in this area also has been felt.

Time to leave the south section and cross the street to the north section. Turn left on Grand River Road and take a right into the graveyard. There will be three trees immediately on the right. Near the tombstones, whispering has been heard and cold spots have been felt.

Continue past the curve, and you will see three trees on the right. There are a few tombstones on either side of these trees. There seems to be a spirit or two in this area that likes to move things. Tape recorders and other similar-sized objects will be moved in this area when you set them down on the ground. They will not be moved far, but imagine your surprise when you set something down for a second, look away and then go to reach for it and it has moved!

Fremont Cemetery has an older, larger section to the south of the road and a smaller, more recent section across the road. Plan a visit and see if you can get a picture of the man leaning on the tombstone. Or if you are inclined, go to the north section and place a small item on the ground, look away and look back to pick it back up. Don't be surprised if it has moved on you.

HILLCREST MEMORIAL GARDENS, OWOSSO

Hillcrest Memorial Gardens is conveniently located just across the street from Oak Hill Cemetery at 1106 South Washington Street. There is only one entrance to the graveyard, and that is located off South Washington Street. There is a big mausoleum; you will see it once you enter the graveyard. The road goes around it. There is a caretaker building on the west side of the graveyard. Trees surround the graveyard on the west, south and north sides, while South Washington is on the east side. The hours are from dawn to dusk.

The first thing you will notice when you drive into the graveyard is on your right. There is a little tree/bush, and against that is a monument, a big, white book open to the Lord's Prayer. There are also two white benches on either side. Right in front of this book, an apparition of a woman has been seen standing; she is looking down, as if in prayer. She quickly disappears after a few seconds.

Follow the road to the mausoleum, which will be right in front of you. In this area, orbs have been seen around the mausoleum as well as a black form that will peek around the corners of the building.

Take a right at the mausoleum and follow it around the curve. There will be tombstones on your right. They look out of place, since there are only a few of them there. You will see four shrubs forming a square, with one shrub at each corner. Keep looking, and you will see one lone tombstone all by itself. Around this lonely tombstone, cold spots have been felt, EVPs have been recorded and orbs have been seen going into the trees.

Head toward the caretaker's building; it should be ahead of you and on the right. Across the road from this building, you will see a cluster of trees on your right with a building among them. I am not sure what the building is used for, though. Near the building, people have reported being scratched on the arm, deep enough to draw blood and raise a welt! If that wasn't enough for you, cold spots have been felt here.

Across the road on your left, you will see a large, empty lot. To the east, there will be some more tombstones and trees. There also will be a building in the area. Look directly east of the building, and you will see a lone tree. In this area, you could possibly hear the sobs of a woman or hear a man's whisper that you can't make out.

Head back toward the mausoleum in the center of the graveyard. To your right, you are looking for a tall tombstone that has "Dynes" on it. By this tombstone, people have felt uneasy and that they shouldn't be in the area.

The feeling of being watched has also been mentioned. Orbs have been seen zigzagging around other tombstones in the area.

Hillcrest Memorial Gardens seems to be a pleasant and well-maintained graveyard. If you drop by one day and happen to see the apparition of the woman by the Lord's Prayer book, give her some peace and quiet; I think she needs it. If you can make out what the man is saying, let me know.

HOWARD CEMETERY, MORRICE

Howard Cemetery is a small graveyard located at 551 West Tyrrell Road There is no road into the graveyard, but there is a little spot where you can park just off the road. The graveyard is surrounded by fields to the west and north, West Tyrrell Road to the south and South Gale Road to the east. While the graveyard is well maintained, there do not appear to be any recent burials. Most of the tombstones date from the 1800s to the early 1900s. The hours are not posted, and since there are no recent burials, I would assume you can be there during reasonable hours.

When you park, look toward the left, and you will see a wire fence. In front of the wire fence, there will be two tombstones. They belong to a husband and wife whose surname was Howard. Since the graveyard is called Howard Cemetery, I wonder if it was named after these people? Cold spots have been felt in this area as well as the feeling of being watched.

A little to the north, you will see four tombstones in a row. They are old and weathered, and you cannot make out what is inscribed on them. An apparition of a man has been seen in the area of these tombstones. He is described as being in his fifties, with white hair. He is wearing a straw hat, button-up plaid shirt, black pants and brown boots.

Howard Cemetery is a nice little graveyard. Even though it appears that no recent burials have taken place, the graveyard is well maintained. If you visit the graveyard and encounter the apparition of the man, ask him if his last name is Howard! Thanks!

LOVEJOY CEMETERY, DURAND

Lovejoy Cemetery doesn't have a physical address, but the graveyard is located on East Prior Road west of South Durand Road, southwest of Durand. The graveyard is surrounded by fields to the south and east. There is one house to the west and East Prior Road to the north. The graveyard is quiet at night; the only sounds you will hear are insects and the occasional wildlife in the area. There are two entrances off East Prior Road. The dates on the tombstones range from the 1800s to the present. The hours are from dawn to dusk.

On August 6, 1903, two trains with the Wallace Brothers Circus were involved in an accident in the city of Durand. The trains contained cars that had animals and performers in them. One of the trains rear-ended the other one. The animals that were killed in the collision, because of their size, were buried near the tracks. The unknown victims are buried in Lovejoy Cemetery. There is an obelisk in the northern section of the graveyard that memorializes the accident. It is hard to read, but the memorial says:

In Memory of the Unknown Dead
Who Lost Their Lives in the
RAILROAD WRECK
of the
GREAT
WALLACE SHOWS
August 6, 1903

Over the years, there have been reports by people who have visited the graveyard of hearing footsteps on the driveway that goes through the graveyard. The footsteps approach them and stop a few feet away. No one can be seen that could be making the footsteps.

If you visit the graveyard in the fall when there are dead leaves on the ground, you can sometimes hear unseen footsteps crunching the leaves as they walk toward you. No one can be seen, and this has happened all through the graveyard.

There is a section in the graveyard that is for infants and children. This section sits on top of a little hill. There have been numerous reports in this section of what has been described as crying, shadows darting between the tombstones and whispers.

There have been sightings of a man in a military uniform standing near the southern end of the graveyard. If you enter the north driveway into the graveyard, follow it around and stop near the road, near a cluster of tombstones, this is where the man has mostly been seen. He is described as wearing what looks like a naval officer's dress uniform. He doesn't move but just stands there and looks straight ahead, then disappears. There are numerous veterans buried in the graveyard, so it is almost impossible to pinpoint who this man could be.

In the center of the graveyard, there have been numerous reports of a woman wearing a long, white dress. She is said to have light brown, shoulder-length hair. She is seen running away from a cluster of tombstones. The bottom of her dress reportedly flows behind her as she runs.

Balls of light have been seen darting in and around the tombstones. The balls of light are normally seen at night with the naked eye. There are no known causes for these balls of light. These balls of light have been seen all over the cemetery and not in just one specific area.

Lovejoy Cemetery is an interesting place during the day but even more interesting after the sun goes down. There are no guarantees that the graveyard will be this active if you choose to visit it. Unfortunately, there isn't a switch you can flip that would turn on the activity. However, the graveyard appears to be quite active; you might just experience one or all the things that have been reported there. If you happen to see the man in the military uniform, thank him for his service before he disappears.

Mount Hope Cemetery, Owosso

Mount Hope Cemetery is one of those graveyards that doesn't rate an actual address on Google Maps. The graveyard is located on North Michigan Street, also known as M-52, just north of West Juddville Road. There are no entrances to the graveyard, but there is a shoulder you can park on across the street. The graveyard is surrounded by trees to the west, West Juddville Road to the south, houses to the north and North Michigan Street to the east. I don't believe there are any new burials here since most of the tombstones appear to be from the 1800s to 1900s and most of them are weathered enough that you cannot read them. The hours are from dawn to dusk.

In the front of the graveyard, you will immediately see one tall tombstone and two smaller ones to the right. In this area, you might get a whiff of lavender, although there are no lavender plants in the area. There have also been reports of smelling cigar smoke when no one is smoking.

On the left side of the graveyard, you will see a tall, granite-colored tombstone that is weathered, with moss growing on it. It is hard to read the name, since it is an older tombstone, but it appears to be "Nonon." Orbs have been seen around this tombstone and going into the trees just to the left.

Near this tombstone is the section of the graveyard that just seems "off."

If you follow the tree line about halfway back to the far end of the graveyard, in this area, EMF meters tend to have spikes that cannot be explained. There are no wires overhead, and I would hope there aren't any wires buried in the graveyard! The area where the spikes occur is only about twenty feet in diameter. If you go outside the area, the EMF meters go quiet; you go back into the area, and the EMF meters come to life.

The overall feeling of this graveyard is a pleasant one. There have been no reports of attacks or anything that could be mistaken for being threatening in nature. However, all that can be thrown out the window in the back corner of the graveyard!

At the far end of the graveyard, near the center and maybe a little to the right, you will find, a few feet in front of the tree line, a tall, granite-colored tombstone that says "Johnson" on it. In this area, things just feel "off." You will feel anxious, sad and that you shouldn't be in this area, all wrapped up in one. And if that wasn't enough for you, there have also been cold spots in this area and the intense feeling of being watched. Growling has also been heard just inside the tree line, and a black shadow has been observed in the same tree line area.

Mount Hope Cemetery is a nice, small and well-kept graveyard. There is a pleasant feeling overall, except for that one section. If you are planning to visit, just remember that there isn't parking in the graveyard; you have to either park on the street right in front or on the shoulder across the street. If you encounter the black shadow in "that" part of the graveyard, see if you can communicate with it and find out what it is doing there. And while you're at it, if you hear the growling in this same area, try and find out what is making that sound. Let me know; I am curious! Thanks in advance.

OAK GROVE CEMETERY, OWOSSO

Oak Grove Cemetery is a small graveyard located at 2820 West Bennington Road. There are two entrances to the graveyard, one off M-52 and the other off West Bennington Road. The graveyard borders M-52 to the west, West Bennington to the south, houses to the north and open land, most likely for expansion, to the east. The tombstones range from the 1800s to the 1900s. The hours are from dawn to dusk.

If you enter the graveyard from West Bennington, you will see a tree directly to your left. Near this tree, there have been cold spots felt, the feeling of being watched and the smell of roses when there aren't any roses in the area.

Look across the road to the east and you will see a bigger tree that sticks out. Under this tree, an apparition of what looks like a farmer has been seen. He has been described as wearing work boots and overalls. He is an older man, possibly in his sixties, with brown hair. He has been seen standing under the tree looking out toward the fields to the west.

A little north of this tree, and to the right a little, is a cluster of tombstones. Around these tombstones, there have been reports of orbs in the area. They usually head in the direction of the empty space to the east and then disappear. There also have been EVPs in this area of a woman's voice and she is saying something along the lines of "Who are you?" There also has been an EVP of a dog barking when there isn't a dog in sight. The sound of the dog sounds like it was close to the tape recorder!

If you follow the road to exit on M-52 you will see a lone tree on your right. In this general area, people have seen a ghost dog. The reports are that the dog is a small one, something 'like either a bulldog or beagle-ish type dog. It is possible that the little dog was killed crossing the road. It is possible that the EVP of the dog barking is this little guy? The dog is always seen running away toward the north.

Toward the north part of the graveyard is a cluster of tombstones. In this area, there have been cold spots that move, feelings of sadness, and a feeling like you are not wanted or welcome in this area. The ghost dog has also been seen running in this area.

Oak Grove Cemetery is a quaint little graveyard and if you're looking for a little something paranormal, this just might be the place for you! If you see the old man under the tree, ask him where his farm used to be. If you happen to see the ghost dog, play a little game of catch with him!

OAK HILL CEMETERY, OWOSSO

Oak Hill Cemetery is located at 1101 South Washington Street. This is a sprawling graveyard that features many mausoleums and a veterans' section, and it even has a good-sized pond on its grounds. The graveyard has many trees on the property, which makes for some very interesting shadows. The graveyard has South Washington and Vandecarr Road to the west, houses to the north and east and trees to the south. The main entrance is off South Washington Road, and there is an entrance off Vandecarr Road. The hours are dawn to dusk.

When you come through the main entrance, you are going to want to stay to your left. You will see a building on your left. Straight ahead in the trees, an apparition of a man has been seen leaning against a tree. You are looking for a tree that has a white sign with the letter *P* written on it. It is nailed to the tree trunk about ten feet off the ground. This isn't the tree

Left: This is the area where an apparition of a man has been seen.

Below: A nice veterans' section; shadows have been seen in and around this area.

you're looking for, though. The tree in question is straight behind the tree with the letter *P*, near the road.

The apparition has been seen leaning with his back against the tree trunk and his right leg bent with his foot resting on the tree trunk also. He is seen wearing blue jeans; a blue, buttoned long-sleeve shirt; cowboy boots; and a baseball hat that is turned backward. You can see him only from a distance; when you start walking toward the tree, he will disappear. When you search the area, no one can be seen.

Keep left on the road, and you will end up in an area that the road forms a square around. In this area, there have been moving cold spots and the feeling of being watched. Look for a couple of trees in the south part of this area; there have been EVPs recorded here that sound like a woman asking for help. A woman's sobbing has been heard a couple of times.

If you move out of this section, about halfway into the next section to the south, you might be lucky enough to have your name called. It seems that some visitors to this section hear what is described as a child's voice calling out their name, and when they look, there isn't anyone there. There have also been reports of people having their pant legs pulled, as if a child were trying to get their attention!

Now, here is where it starts to get a little interesting and maybe a whole lot of fun! Head west from the area where you have been, toward South Washington road. If this is any help, there will be a veterans' section just to the north. Here you will find a mausoleum. There are two side by side, but the one of interest is the one for Bentley. There are round door knockers on both doors to the mausoleum, which unfortunately don't open. Legend has it that if you use the door knockers and knock twice, you will hear two knocks in reply coming from inside the closed mausoleum.

Walk the short distance north to the veteran's section. This is a pretty cool thing they have done! There is a flagpole—flying Old Glory, of course—and there are rows of veterans' tombstones moving away from the flagpole. Shadows, not actually apparitions or shadow people, have been seen moving around the veterans' tombstones.

Oak Hill Cemetery seems to have some visitors that come and make their presence known, and they are not the alive kind. I am sure there are more active spots in the graveyard and not just the ones listed above. If you experience any activity not listed above, please let me know! If you can get close enough to the apparition of the man leaning against the tree, find out his name. I am always curious about this type of thing. If you try knocking at the door of the mausoleum and you get a reply back, let me know. And finally, if you see the spirit of a veteran, thank him for his service!

SAINT PAUL'S CEMETERY, OWOSSO

Saint Paul's Cemetery is located at 1677 South Chipman Street. Here is another example that makes one scratch one's head. The address is South Chipman Street, and Google Maps has it off West South Street. But if you look at the map, the graveyard borders both streets, so there you go. There is an entrance off West South Street and two off South Morrice Road. The graveyard borders South Chipman Street to the west, and there are houses to the south, an open field to the east and West South Street to the north. The hours are from dawn to dusk.

Take the entrance off West South Street, take the right and just past the curb on your left in this area, a transparent apparition of a little boy has been observed. He has been seen running in between the tombstones and then he will just fade away.

Up ahead on the left, you will see what looks like a blue spruce. Just to the left of the tree, there will be three tombstones. In this area, electronic equipment will fail, and batteries will be drained; when you leave the area, the batteries are fully charged again. Orbs have been seen in this area, and cold spots have been felt.

If you continue straight and take a left at the intersection, you will come to the graveyard version of a roundabout. In front of you should be a monument erected by the Knights of Columbus No. 1139; it says:

In Loving Memory of
God's Unborn
Children

In this area, there have been reports of people hearing a child quietly weeping. I don't know if this is the power of suggestion, but this sound has reportedly been heard.

If you take the first "exit" off the roundabout, you will see a tree right in front of you. To the right of the tree, there will be a cluster of tombstones. Unexplained noises—what sounds like a piece of steel hitting concrete and footsteps—have been heard on the road under the tree, even though no one is walking on the road.

If you go forward, take the first left and continue until the road comes to a *T*. There will be five or so tombstones right alongside the road. There have been voices heard coming from the trees across the road. Pictures have also been taken that have unexplained streaks of light in them.

Turn right and take the next right. There will be seven pine trees on your left. Across the road from these trees, there have been reports of feeling watched, an uneasy feeling and getting goosebumps. An EVP was recorded in this area years ago. It was of a man's voice, which in a whisper asked, "Am I buried?"

Go past the curve and take a left to leave the graveyard. Just before you leave the graveyard and hit South Chipman Street, you will see a row of trees next to the road. Right in front, there will be nine tombstones in a row. In and around these tombstones, orbs have been seen and cold spots felt. At the farthest tombstone to the north, pictures have captured what looks like ectoplasmic mist.

Saint Paul's Cemetery is a good-sized graveyard where one could spend hours just walking around and looking at the different styles of tombstones and monuments. If you happen to see the apparition of the boy, ask him if wants to play hide and go seek!

ABOUT THE AUTHOR

B radley P. Mikulka has been conducting investigations with his group, the Southeast Michigan Ghost Hunters Society, since 1996. He has investigated hundreds of locations across America and Europe. He grew up in a haunted house, so he has a unique take on the paranormal. His group has appeared on the TV show *A Haunting* and the DVD *A Haunting on Hamilton Street*.

Visit us at
www.historypress.com